What is required is a judicious evaluation of the historical development of the American seminary, of its present structure and goals, and of its imperative future modernization—an evaluation based not on some well-intentioned or second-hand sentiments about aggiornamento, but on a sense of concrete history and on practical experience in educating seminarians.

Father Poole is a historian, holding the Ph.D. degree from St. Louis University, the former Vice-rector of Cardinal Glennon College, St. Louis, and presently Dean of Studies at St. Mary's Seminary, Perryville, Mo. SEMINARY IN CRISIS is a book which recognizes the complexity of the difficulties faced by present-day seminary administrators and faculties who often must cope with a continental educational regime, with a shortage of trained personnel, with an isolated cultural atmosphere, with students whose high-minded goals are themselves a cause of increased psychological tensions. Father Stafford Poole examines specifically the qualifications for seminary faculties, the role of the seminary administration, the character of the modern seminarian, his spiritual and intellectual training, and his attitude towards obedience and authority. The book concludes with a description of "the seminary of Utopia," the seminary reunited with the university, nurturing and being nurtured by it, and thus becoming a genuine training ground for the priest who must exercise his ministry in the world.

As Bishop John King Mussio points out in his enthusiastic foreword to SEMINARY IN CRISIS, the work of forming young priests is a work of the whole people of God. It is a work which must be understood and fostered by the laity, by members of the religious orders, as well as by the clergy. This book, like the seminaries it treats of, is of importance to Catholics on all levels of the Church.

The need for radically improving the formation of future priests has been acknowledged almost universally: discerning critics both among the laity and the clergy have repeatedly pointed out the consequences of a priestly education which is not adapted to the pastoral needs of the present age of the Church. But it would be as naive to think that every Catholic, or even every priest, is qualified to discuss seminary reform as to imagine that every college graduate is by that fact qualified to discuss the changing role of the American university. What is required, now that there is a widespread concern with effective priestly formation, is certainly not more and more cataloging of defects in the training of recent generations of priests, nor more and more complaints about the existing seminary system—at this late date a mere re-stating or over-stating of the terms of the problem is to make no real contribution to its solution. That phase of the question is passed.

Seminary in Crisis

SEMINARY IN CRISIS

Stafford Poole C.M.

HERDER AND HERDER

1965
HERDER AND HERDER NEW YORK
232 Madison Avenue, New York 10016

Library of Congress Catalog Card Number: 65-20558
© 1965 by Herder and Herder, Incorporated
Printed in the United States of America

CONTENTS

Author's Note   9
Foreword   11
1. The Changing Seminary   18
2. The Historical Context   30
3. Canonical Organization   56
4. Today's Seminarian   66
5. The Faculty and the Environment   75
6. Intellectual Standards and Curriculum   95
7. Spiritual Formation   121
8. Of Freedom and Obedience   136
9. The Seminary of Utopia   156
Appendix: Thoughts on the Problem
   of Perseverance   164

Dedicated with admiration and respect to all those who are engaged in any way in the work of seminaries.

No matter how we seek, we shall always discover ourselves unable to contribute to anything greater than the formation of a good priest.

Vincent de Paul

Author's Note

It is impossible to pay tribute to all those who have contributed in any way to this book. I would like to thank globally all my fellow Vincentians whose constant support, encouragement, and constructive criticism is the only thing that kept me at work on this project through several dark hours. Specifically, I would like to thank Father Francis Gaydos C.M., S.T.D., who has waged a long unheralded battle for seminary improvement; Father Robert Coerver C.M., S.T.D., for his initial encouragement and help with the article on which this book is based; Father Thomas Feeley C.M., M.A., Ph.D., for valuable suggestions on the reform of minor orders; Father Gilmore Guyot C.M., S.T.L., S. Scr. B., Father Joseph Cozy C.M., J.C.L., Father Joseph Bronars C.M., Ph.D., Father John Lavanway C.M., M.A., and Father Bruce Vawter C.M., S.T.D., SS.D.

Also I would like to acknowledge the progressive suggestions of Father John Byrne, Ph.D., of St. Louis; Father Eugene Kennedy M.M., Ph.D., of Maryknoll Seminary, Glen Ellyn, Illinois; Father Eugene Burke C.S.P., S.T.D., of St. Paul's College, Washington, D.C.; Father Andrew Greeley M.A., Ph.D., of Chicago; Monsignor John Tracy Ellis,

Ph.D., of the University of San Francisco; Father Christopher Huntington of St. Pius X Minor Seminary, Rockville Center; and two of my former students, Mr. Joseph Foy, M.A., and Mr. William Kerr, of Theological College, Washington, D.C., for valuable insights on the student's point of view; and Mr. Justus George Lawler, my editor. Lastly, I would like to thank my provincial, Father James Fischer C.M., S.T.L., S.S.L., whose own tolerance created the climate in which this book could be written.

Foreword

Whether we like the idea or not, change means change. There is no significance whatsoever to *aggiornamento* unless we understand the word as defined in the Johannine lexicon: modernization, renewal, a stepping into the twentieth century. As applied to the Church, it signifies an effective assistance to her in the fulfillment of her mission to serve people everywhere. This means an assistance whereby the Church brings Christ to the flock not as someone strange and unknown, but as One who knows his own in the smallest detail of their living, and loves them enough to be concerned in that smallest detail. The only way the people of God are to see this Christ is in the Church. How the Church appears to them is exactly what Christ means to them. What she says, how she acts, the keenness of her interest in everyday living, her sharp insight into the problems that beset twentieth-century man, the readiness and sureness with which she meets the challenges to Christian order and morality, all of this determines the place of the Church in the scale of values honored by this world of ours today.

It is entirely unrealistic to expect old patterns of thought

and practice to meet a situation which has not developed
through the slow and step-by-step movement that characterized the past, but has simply exploded us into an entirely new age. The technological, economic, scientific,
industrial, sociological, and philosophical advances which
have characterized this age can be classified only as revolutionary. They are all for the good as long as those who
know the Truth keep all things in good order. There is no
question of a change in the Church that would change the
unchangeable truth—no one of a God-centered heritage
would hold otherwise or want otherwise. This basic fact
must be understood if anything at all is to be understood
in the light of John's *aggiornamento*.

The priest as the pastor of souls is the Church in action.
He is the hand of Christ that reaches out to the flock
making the Savior a living reality in their lives. The
Church moves in the life of this twentieth century only
as the priest knows his people, their ways, their problems,
needs, worries, hopes, and expectations. He must be one
of his flock. Basically, this means he must be a man of his
age. The renewal of the Church depends, in the last
analysis, on the priest knowing what it is all about. The
Council Fathers at present are working on a text which
considers the place of the priest in the work of the Church.
The time is past to overlook the *indispensable* service of
the priest in the mission of the Church. The priest stands
in his own right, not as in the shadow of others. No matter
how inspired the vision of the Supreme Pontiff, or how
justified and necessary the plans of the bishop, nothing

can effectively be done without the priest and that certain indispensability he has from Christ for the perfection of Christian action. If the Church is to walk in this twentieth century, it is going to be on the strong and determined legs of the priest. The Council Fathers, bishops from all over the world, know well that no matter what the Council decrees, it will remain but a printed text unless the priest, by the performance of his ordained duty, transforms it into the flesh and blood of a Christian incentive to change things into the living Image of the living God.

It is not fair to place such a responsibility on the priest without preparing him for the right fulfillment of this charge. To know man, you must know his time; to know his problems, you must know his challengers; to sound the depths of his discouragement, you must know something of his aims and objectives; to feel his fears, you must see the ghosts that rise up before him. And so, too, to be a shepherd, you must know your flock, know each one by his name and by those distinguishing marks that make him yours. It is the responsibility of the Church to prepare the priest to be "knowing," to be a man of this world inasmuch as this worldliness makes him a better shepherd of his people. That priest must walk into his work with the full confidence of a proper preparation.

Because of this responsibility that lies with the Church, the Council Fathers have discussed and are now revising for final voting and promulgation the schema which is concerned with the training of the future priest. They recognize that this is of utmost importance to the entire

Church. Underlying the thought of this schema is the conviction that the seminarian of today is the product of his age. If he is so secluded from his world that he becomes a stranger to it, then he has been successfully trained in uselessness. A seminarian who has been so formed that he becomes indifferent to the world and to its problems is one betrayed in his own calling. If the seminarian is to go out into this world as a priest prepared to make Christ effective in all that a man does and thinks, then he must be trained to know his world, to know what constitutes modern man, and to know how to present Christ's message so that it makes sense to one who sees so much senselessness about him. An isolated seminarian means a detached priest; and clerical detachment from our people and from our time has given rise to much that is called anticlericalism, but which in reality is nothing more than the strangeness of estrangement. A seminarian developed in the traditions, the thought, the monastic atmosphere of centuries past will be lost in an age in which antiquities are curios. A seminarian who has never been disciplined in the proper use of those freedoms which are entirely compatible with his priestly calling becomes a priest who is himself so confused in his confrontation with the world that he has no time or strength to take on the cares of others. A seminarian whose creative yet disciplined thinking is squashed in the seminary is a priest who can give no constructive help to his bishop in facing positively modern challenges. The Church knows this, the bishops know this, the priest knows this, and the seminarian knows this. And here, for one moment, I would like to digress.

Much today is said and worried about dropouts from the seminary. There seems to be no one pattern in the withdrawals. For my part, I believe that many of these seminarians leave because they are honest, intelligent, and conscientious men who have a keen insight as to what will be expected of them as spiritual leaders, yet at the same time are conscious of the fact that they are unprepared to meet the challenge. In them we see our failure, not theirs. Seminarians are the children of today, they know their time better than we who are older. Only when the seminary training gives them the confidence of being equipped properly to face the demands of today's spiritual needs will they be freed from the compulsions which today often result in a regretful withdrawal.

Progress is nothing but new ideas improving on old ones. Any place, any time ideas are proscribed, there progress is stymied. There are good ideas and there are bad ideas, there are ideas that would destroy progress and there are those without which our world would stagnate. Choking off ideas kills the good ones as well as the bad, harms progress as well as promotes stagnation. In this age of trained minds, the duty of the Church is to show which ideas are for the good of man and the welfare of his world. The Church has nothing to fear from ideas. She has the Truth, and with that Truth the standard by which she can separate the good from the bad. And even among the good ideas, there are various grades of excellence and effectiveness. The Church, then, must encourage thinking that produces the best in ideas, the kind of thinking that will serve best the fulfillment of her divine mission. And our today certainly needs new and pertinent ideas that will get the job done better.

And so we come to the positive contribution of Father Stafford Poole's book, *Seminary in Crisis*, to the implementation of conciliar thought in the life of our times. It is a contribution to progress by a presentation of ideas for the improvement of seminary life and training. There are some who would leave the seminary as it is, others who think there should be a radical change. Each is entitled to his view. But no one should close himself to new ideas presented in the best interests of the training of our future priests. Father Poole is a man who knows his subject through close experience and from long years of observation made through sympathetic yet expert eyes. He is a man who loves what the seminary stands for, and is dedicated to all that is best for an effective and significant product. The author does not demand the acceptance of his ideas or of his plans. He thinks, however, that they deserve attention, and so do I. He respects the rights of others to present their ideas on the subject. It is this interchange of ideas which in the end will produce a plan for seminary life and training that will satisfy the best conciliar thinking on the subject. One thing I think should be stressed: we must not sniff at any idea presented unless we can show its falsity or, if mediocre, present a better one. We can take it as certain that nothing good will be brought about unless men of Father Poole's devotion to a productive seminary training come forth and speak. I am convinced that books such as *Seminary in Crisis* are the best guarantee we have that the spirit of the Second Vatican Council is catching on, and that the *aggiornamento* of Pope John as well as the spirit of his successor, Pope Paul, is beginning to open doors in our modern world. Reading such a book as *Seminary in Crisis* does not mean necessarily that one will agree with all that is said. The author does not expect this. But it does mean that one will be stimulated to think about what must be thought about if the priest of tomorrow is to show the fruit of a training that opens rather than closes his mind to the world we are living in.

† JOHN KING MUSSIO
BISHOP OF STEUBENVILLE

1

The Changing Seminary

There is a good deal of ferment in seminaries today. When seminary administrators gather to discuss common problems, it immediately becomes evident that a sort of new wave is sweeping through the student bodies of seminaries in America. No matter what the institution, the problems seem largely the same. A new generation with new problems has descended on us, and many persons in authority feel both confused and vaguely apprehensive. It is all too easy to dismiss this ferment of ideas as a peculiar aberration of today's seminarians—the result of too much freedom, of a worldly environment, or of too gullible an acceptance of ideas and suggestions from the outer fringes of contemporary Catholic thought. For these problems stubbornly refuse to vanish, and to speak disparagingly of the "spoiled youth of today" or of "the insidious spirit of independence and novelty" is to beg the question altogether. The function of seminary teachers and administrators is to close the gap between the positive and specific ideal of the priesthood and the student *as he is*.

There is about us today a bewildering variety of approaches and suggestions, some of which are advocated as theories, others of which have already been put into practice. Many represent genuine progress, others may be fads. There are some priests who feel that changes in the seminary must proceed with a maximum of deliberation and slowness. After all, they reason, the seminary as it is now has proven its effectiveness by the graduates it has turned out over the past decades, whereas any changes that are made will require generations to prove themselves. The presumption of effectiveness favors the seminary which has served the Church so well for so long. The proponents of this view argue that there is too much at stake to take chances on experiments.

But is the seminary effective? Are the methods that produced good priests in 1930 or 1940 pertinent to the world of the 1960s or, more important, of the 1970s, -80s, and -90s? The current agitation about anticlericalism and clerical-lay tensions cannot be dismissed as the vagary of an extremist intellectual fringe.[1] There is a very definite and growing groundswell of dissatisfaction with the clergy, and it can be countered effectively in only one area, within the clergy itself. Because the seminary, like any living body, must grow and adapt, it must strain the limits of human ability to look into the future into which it is going to send the next few generations of Catholic priests. It cannot be content to look back nostalgically to the past and its accomplishments.

The disheartening truth is that we really have no idea how effective the seminary is. Priests have expressed their dissatisfaction with the training they have received, and this frequently in magazines and journals which have a wide lay readership.[2] More startling is the conclusion reached by a news magazine of international circulation:

Some Church leaders believe that American Catholicism is heading for a crisis in authority. Many bishops are worried about the number of potentially good priests who leave seminaries rather than submit to picayune rules and a dry, unappealing curriculum. Younger priests chafe under an archaic system that puts them completely at the mercy of pastors. . . . There are reportedly between 4,000 and 5,000 priests who have left the clergy in the U.S. with frustration high among their reasons.[3]

If these statements are even partially true, then the seminary is indeed carrying a heavy burden. How accurate is the estimate of the number of priestly defections? No one knows for sure. Yet if some data on this were available, the American Church would have an idea as to whether seminary training is really effective and might be able to find some clues as to its weakness. It is a distasteful topic and one that should not be exaggerated, but the central issue must be faced.

The same is true of the rate of alcoholism among priests and the extent to which it disables otherwise worthy men. It has been estimated that the rate is higher than the national average, yet there are no reliable statistics. Again, such data might give us a clue as to what the weaknesses of the seminary are. What about disabling mental disturbances? To what extent have they ever been studied among the clergy? In 1961, McAllister and Vandervelt discovered that "there was a greater number of sociopathic personality disturbances" among hospitalized Catholic clergy than among comparable groups of laymen. Of one hundred hospitalized Catholic priests investigated, forty-six showed evidence of lifelong mental disturbance, that is, of difficulties which could have been discovered in the seminary.[4] Other studies have indicated that the seminary and religious environment is attractive and congenial to passive and sexually confused personalities.[5]

It must, of course, be said that information such as this tells us nothing of the good work being done by thousands of dedicated but unrecognized priests throughout the nation. From immigration through middle-class acceptance, the American Catholic has been served by his clergy as few peoples of modern times have been. Priests took the lead in helping the newly arrived immigrant adjust to his strange and hostile environment and to americanize himself and his family. The result has been an extremely close relationship between priest and flock and an unusually high degree of loyalty and religious practice by the average Catholic. But, as Vincent de Paul has said, the good is frequently the enemy of the better.

It is all too easy to rest content with past accomplishments and to avoid the unpleasant necessity of foreseeing approaching difficulties. Some idea of the disabling factors in the priesthood would certainly help give the seminaries a sense of direction and an idea of what they are combating. Moreover, every priest incapacitated by one of the problems mentioned above could probably be matched with one whose sexual confusions have been borne without outside professional help, by one whose ignorance has wreaked havoc in the confessional or counseling parlor, and by one who is lazy, indifferent, frustrated, or just defeated by it all.

Let us put these questions aside and concentrate on the normal priest. We shall find that he is facing a world which is undergoing revolutionary change, for the trends and movements within the Church are now reaching the ordinary layman, even through the mass media. Liturgy, the new theology and scriptural studies, social and racial problems, population and family planning, the increased education and sophistication of the laity, the changing population structure and the problems of the inner city, the loosening of family ties and the confusion of roles in the modern family—today's parish priest is faced with problems that were hardly thought of twenty years ago. And there is every indication that these problems will grow in number and complexity rather than diminish.[6]

In view of this, the seminary must play a twofold role: 1) to train a man for tasks that are specifically priestly, what we might call his professional training; and 2) to educate, a function that the seminary has in common with all schools. The latter touches on the seminarian precisely as a man, the former under the aspect of his special vocation. It would be dangerous to suppose that there is any intrinsic contradiction between the two. Obviously, anything that perfects an individual as man is going to help him in his vocation as priest. A few latter-day Jansenists would have us believe that the human side is beyond hope and that divine grace, alone and unaided, will effect the formation of a good clergy;

while some contemporary Pelagians would have us believe that all seminarians are so thoroughly noble that by themselves they will accomplish all that is necessary to be a good priest.

Whatever improves the man improves the priest. And because a vocation is a gift granted to a man, what improves himself precisely as priest improves him as a human being.

Unhappily, the role of the diocesan priest in the United States has often been the subject of confusion. It cannot be doubted that to the layman the image of the parish priest suffers in comparison with that of the religious, especially if the latter belongs to a teaching order. There is a general, if often unspoken, assumption that the religious is more intelligent, better trained, a better preacher, and generally more proficient in counseling and spiritual direction. The diocesan priesthood lacks the glamour of the missionary life and of traditions descending from canonized holy founders and from the *esprit de corps* of the organization. In the appendix, we shall discuss this same difficulty in relation to perseverance in the seminary.

This same confusion about the role of the parish priest is shared by the laity. As Daniel Callahan has described it:

It is by no means clear that the contemporary educated Catholic layman knows exactly what he wants. Most commonly he will speak of the need for more communication between laity and clergy; for greater responsibility; for freedom from clerical paternalism; for a clerical recognition that the temporal order cannot be scorned or degraded or the world denied. . . . Yet at the same time he may complain that the clergy do not tell him what to do in the world; that neither priests nor bishops provide

him with sufficient guidance and direction to enable him to
cope with the modern age. This ambivalence—between a desire
to be free and a desire to be led—is rarely absent from even the
most sophisticated writing and speaking by laymen.[7]

Nor is this attitude lacking in the seminary. Administrators and faculties can agree in general about the kind of
priest they consider desirable, but when it is a question of
particulars, the agreement ceases. Everyone wants intelligent priests, but how intelligent? Everyone wants zealous
priests, but what about the under-achiever? Everyone wants
a good preacher, but what about the student who cannot be
heard in the back pew, even with the aid of a loudspeaker?

In seeking answers to these and similar questions, we have
followed some general principles concerning the qualities
that priests of the immediate future will need.

Intellectual Adaptability. In a revolutionary age, this quality is indispensable for leadership. Without it, a man will
sink into utter superficiality or blind reaction. The limitless
ability shown by man, whether in the Church or out of it,
to resist progressive, healthy, and necessary movements is
certainly one of the more dismaying lessons of history. The
situation of the Catholic Church in many Latin countries,
also the example of many modern churchmen, amply dem-
onstrates the tragic results of frozen attitudes, closed minds,
and the inability to separate accidentals from essentials.
Conversely, in more recent times, we see the same fault at
work in those who automatically take up every new idea
merely and precisely because it is new. The priest in his lifetime faces a dazzling variety of personalities and parish situ-

ations that call for a high degree of adaptability and insight.

Intellectual Achievement. Adaptability is a useless virtue to an ignorant man. The work of the priesthood presupposes and demands broad intellectual achievement, and it is one of the premises of this book that it cannot be attained by anyone who is not capable of achieving at least a bachelor's degree in an accredited college. The premise is important, for there is a strong anti-intellectual sentiment among many priests who extol more "human" qualities at the expense of intellectual excellence, originality, and creativeness.

Liturgical Understanding. By ordination, the priest is a liturgist in the full and proper sense of the term. His own life must be formed around the principles of the liturgy. He must communicate the life of the Church to others, both as celebrant of the Christian mysteries and as the dispenser of the word of God—through him the faithful are brought into contact with both the incarnate and the inspired word.

A Modern Man. Again, this is a phrase to be taken in its full and proper sense. The priest should be familiar with the contemporary bent and its genuine aspirations and criticisms. He should understand the bases and background of modern American life and should be able to attempt an understanding of the crises of each generation he encounters. He should be well grounded in the behavioral and social sciences as a means of understanding his parishioners.

When these principles are coupled with practical suggestions, it is hoped that they will help to clarify the image of what a priest should be. Of course, they do not reach to the essence of the priestly office, for our concern is not to offer a theological treatise on the priesthood, but to indicate ways for fuller and more effective compenetration by priests into the world they serve.

If the image of the diocesan priest is vague, that of the seminary is usually nonexistent. It is no exaggeration to say that for most people a seminary is a place where priests are trained—and that is all that they know about it. Even for young men who are thinking of the priesthood, the years between their vocational decision and their eventual ordination loom as a gigantic question mark. But for others the seminary is an outrage. Lytton Strachey shuddered at the thought of the introduction into England of the Roman seminary and its "grim perspective of espionage and tale-bearing, foreign habits, and Italian devotions." Daniel Callahan has flailed them as isolated, reactionary, and suffocating. John Lancaster Spalding, the first Bishop of Peoria, put his finger on a major weakness when he said: "The ecclesiastical seminary is not a school of intellectual culture, either here in America or elsewhere, and to imagine that it can become the instrument of intellectual culture is to cherish a delusion."[8] The other extreme can be found in the recent instructions from the Sacred Congregation of Seminaries and Universities which showed great satisfaction with the status quo and which, apparently, suggested by implication that any advance beyond the eighteenth century was a step in the wrong direction.[9]

This book is not intended to be the last word or even an

approximation of it on the problem of seminaries. It cannot claim to be an exhaustive treatment of them, neither does it make any pretense of being a work of scholarship. It is simply an attempt to consider in a rational way the problems facing the seminary in our country today and to formulate some solutions.

Therefore, we shall avoid any stale generalization or condemnation or platitude that has become almost the trademark of much of today's writing on *aggiornamento*. But when an idea is proposed, it is offered to stand or fall on its own intrinsic merits. These pages are designed to stimulate discussion, thought, and action by the men who are now conducting Catholic seminaries in the United States, and by all who are concerned in any way with priestly formation.

The ideas proposed are of unequal value. Many will come to nothing, but they should be accepted for what they are: serious proposals, open for discussion, not to be condemned because they are different nor embraced for the same reason. There is true value in defending what we have, for then we know why we should want to keep it.

This book is directed first and foremost to seminary administrators and faculties—and particularly to the central figure in all seminary administration, the bishop. These are the men on the front lines, those most closely and intimately associated with the enormous task of preparing men for ordination and ministry.

But we have also had in mind seminarians, parish priests, and laity. The formation of priests is a work of the whole Christian community, even though the proximate task may devolve on a minority. It is something which concerns the entire Church and in which the entire Church should have a share and a voice. For these groups, seminarians, parish priests, laity, it is our special hope that this effort will help to illuminate some of the complexities of seminary work. The training of priests is an impossible, tedious, frustrating, irritating, and occasionally rewarding task. It is unique. And it is all too easy to criticize from the sidelines without realizing the scope of the problems involved. Seminarians in particular have a maddening habit of reading uncritically works such as this and then demanding the full and immediate implementation of all the suggestions offered.

Our subject is the diocesan seminaries of the United States. Religious seminaries are not considered. We have restricted ourself to this country because the situation here is complex enough, and because, obviously, it is impossible to establish a suitable, international, uniform educational system. Neither shall we discuss, except incidentally, the minor or high school seminary. Our focus point is the years of college and theology.

The thesis of this book is that if the seminary is to keep abreast of the modern world, it is going to have to be reunited organically with lay education. Without losing its distinctive character as a professional school, the seminary must return to the university as an integral part, influencing and being influenced by it. This assumption underlies all the suggestions that are made in the following pages, and even when alternate suggestions are made, the former is always the ideal. And like any ideal, this also will not be realized easily, or by delay.

Finally, parenthetically, we should state categorically that the seminary system of the United States is the Achilles' Heel of American Catholicism.[10] All the thought, all the struggle, all the dedication that have gone into the cause of renewal in our land may well have been expended uselessly if it never reaches the parochial level under the leadership of the clergy. Unless the training of priests keeps pace with other developments within the Church, then renewal will either remain the province of a minority, or else the layman's frustrated zeal will cause him to reject the guidance of the clergy altogether, and not without cause.

Improvement and modernization of the seminary system will succeed only if actual inspiration, actual direction, and actual leadership come from the bishops. To them has been entrusted the chief responsibility for the training of priests, and they alone, acting together, can insure for generations to come a living priesthood that is once again a dynamic element of the Christian world, and at the same time encourage and not destroy the hope for seminary renewal of so many of our own day.

2

The Historical Context

I

The story of clerical education, from the foundation of the Church until the time of the Council of Trent, is a cyclical one of alternate decline and reform. All too often this reform was superficial, local, or failed entirely to cure the chronic problem that has afflicted the Church throughout much of its history—unworthy and ineffective ministers.[1]

Every seminarian has been told at some time or another that the first seminary consisted of Christ and his apostles. What he may not be told is that, like its successors, the first was not entirely successful and certainly did not have complete perseverance. But it did set the pattern for one vital element in the subsequent training of priests, namely strong reliance on a personal contact between teacher and pupil. Instruction was based on a master-disciple relationship and it was experiential, oral, and traditional. The most effective pedagogical tool was example, and learning came by apprenticeship. Paul and Titus, Paul and Timothy, John and Polycarp and Irenaeus, Ambrose and Augustine—the

history of the early Church tells of many similar examples.

From the beginning, the Church had a well defined organizational structure, though on a far smaller scale than now. The bishop's rule was identified with the city where he lived, for Christians were a predominantly urban people. He was *the* preacher for the Christian community, and many of his functions were no different from those of a modern pastor. The number of priests was small—in 250 A.D., Rome had only forty-six priests—and their duties were mostly in the way of liturgical and pastoral assistance to the bishop. The early Church had no specific institution for the training of priests.[2] Rhetorical or literary skills were not considered essential. When in the second century Justin founded his school in Rome, he did not intend it to be a training center for priests. The same was true of the later schools of Alexandria and Antioch. Though they attempted, in a way that seems primitive to us today, to inculcate an encyclopedic knowledge of all disciplines, they were not seminaries. Actually, very few priests seem to have been graduated from them, and the content of clerical education for many centuries was to remain entirely catechetical—the reading and explaining of Scripture, preparing catechumens for baptism, learning to administer the sacraments. The principal means of training the clergy seems to have been through the exercise of the minor orders.[3]

Augustine was probably the first to attempt to impose a type of communal life on aspirants for the priesthood. He established in Hippo a residence where his priests and those desiring to be priests were obliged to live, and where candidates for the priesthood would have the opportunity to study and absorb the spirit of their vocation. It was basically an improvement of the apprentice system, but it did not provide any systematic training of the prospective priest. However, it had become a rather widespread institution throughout Western Europe by the time of the dissolution of the Roman Empire.

All the positive accomplishments of the Church in bringing both the faith and the remnants of classical civilization to the Germanic barbarians, and the successor states which they founded on the ruins of the Western Empire, were adversely affected by the break-up of European civilization. The training and learning of the clergy suffered in a special way. Gregory of Tours is typical of the decline of the once glorious literary culture of the classical world.[4] The Carolingian Revival affected only a temporary alleviation of this sorry situation, at least outside the British Isles, but even this revival was all but extinguished by the new waves of barbarian invasions that swept over Western Europe in the ninth and tenth centuries.[5]

This period saw the almost total degradation of the Church. In Rome the papacy passed under the control of the House of Theophylact and the Roman nobility, with unfortunate results both for the Holy See and the Church at large. Clerical education soon was unheard-of as the old apprentice system broke down almost completely. Concubinage, simony, absenteeism, political control were only the more prominent vices of the day.

The great reform movement that originated with the

foundation of the monastery of Cluny in 950 brought about a notable improvement. However, as a movement, the Cluniac Reform was not intended to establish a system of popular clerical education, and the percentage of priests on whom it had a direct impact was small. This reform coincided with the feudalization of the Church. Feudalism, the peculiar socioeconomic-military structure of the Middle Ages, had its counterpart in the Church which, as part of the European picture, could not help being affected by its environment. It particularly influenced the Church by its emphasis on the hierarchical and monarchical structure of Church government, an emphasis that found its greatest expression in the papal monarchy and in the work of such men as Gregory VII, Boniface VIII, and Innocent III.

With the restoration of political stability and with cultural growth came the renewal of education, particularly in the monastic and cathedral schools. In these latter, especially, the Church had for the first time a means of training her clergy, both in the theological sciences and in the standard literary education of the day. But these schools offered only limited opportunity for any studies besides the rudimentary lessons of grammar and rhetoric.[6] The cathedral schools were eclipsed by the rise of the great universities, where theology was the ruling science. These were in a real sense religiously oriented, but this did not mean that they were ideally suited for the training of the clergy.

It is a bit difficult to determine exactly how the clergy of those centuries received their training for the priesthood since it seems that only a slight percentage of them were able to pursue

their studies at the university. For this latter minority, colleges
or boarding schools were established near the universities themselves. The young candidates for Holy Orders lived a common
life in these institutions provided for that purpose. At the beginning the young clerical students were closely guarded in
these colleges, but, as time went on, the good discipline maintained there for a while disappeared. Consequently, in less than
a century, the life of ecclesiastical students at the universities
was no better than that of the lay students. Even though these
privileged few enjoyed high intellectual advantages, they received little or no spiritual training. What they really lacked was
character formation, moral discipline, and a practical preparation for the ministry.[7]

Since only a small fraction of the medieval clergy could
attend these universities, the vast majority was still being
spawned in a system that had not changed substantially in
a thousand years—or worse, they were not exposed to any
system at all. For a second time, the stage was set for decline and reform.

By 1500 the condition of the papacy and of the clergy
had again sunk to such a low level that only a catastrophic
rending of the unity of the Church was able to bring about
the long-needed reform. As the undercurrent of anticlericalism and antipapalism that had run so strongly through the
Middle Ages burst into the open, the Church came to
realize that all attempts at widespread reform were inher-
ently defective unless accompanied by a more limited reform that would begin with the clergy—from the lowliest
curate to the Pope himself.

An interesting insight into the condition of the pre-tridentine clergy is to be found in the writings of Vincent de
Paul. Ordained at the age of nineteen, before the decrees of

Trent had been promulgated in France, Vincent was in a particularly advantageous position to assess the character of the French clergy. Toward the end of his life he wrote:

Oh, if you had seen, I will not say merely the ugliness, but the diversity of the ceremonies of the Mass forty years ago, they would have made you ashamed. It seems to me that there is nothing uglier in the world than the different ways in which Mass used to be celebrated; some began the Mass with the *Pater Noster*; others took hold of the chasuble, said the *Introibo*, and then put on the chasuble. I was once at Saint-Germain-en-Laye and I remarked seven or eight priests who all said Mass differently; this one did it one way, that another; there was such diversity as to make one weep.[8]

"They [diocesan priests] were so ignorant of our mysteries," wrote Courtin, the biographer of Adrien Bourdoise (whom Vincent credited as being the first to realize the necessity of seminaries), "that some were met with who did not even know Jesus Christ and could not say how many natures there were in him. . . . Many administered the sacraments in Church clad in a doublet." Wise penitents, such as Louise de Marillac, habitually carried the formula of penitential absolution with them, for the benefit of ignorant confessors. Pascal summarized the situation in his statement: "He is made a priest who wants to be."

It was against this background that the Council of Trent decreed the establishment of seminaries in July of 1563 in chapter 28 of the twenty-third session. It declared that all cathedral and metropolitan churches and those greater than these "shall be bound, each according to its means and the extent of its diocese, to provide for, to educate in religion, and to train in ecclesiastical discipline, a certain number of boys of their city and diocese, or, if they are not found there, of their province, in a college located near the said churches or in some other suitable place to be chosen by the bishop." The students to be received into these seminaries were to be "at least twelve years of age, . . . born of lawful wedlock, who know how to read and write competently, and whose character and inclination justify the hope that they will dedicate themselves forever to the ecclesiastical ministry."[9]

The Council did not go into detail about the length or nature of this training, other than to say that the bishop should divide the students into as many classes as necessary and, when necessary, assign them to pastoral work in the churches. From the beginning, they were to wear the tonsure and the ecclesiastical garb and were to be thoroughly trained in religious subjects. Their spiritual exercises were to be the daily sacrifice of the Mass, with Communion at the discretion of their confessors, monthly confession, and service at the solemn ceremonies in the cathedral on holy days.

Thus the specifics of priestly training as outlined by Trent are scant, most of them being left to the discretion of the bishop.[10] Interestingly enough, almost three-fourths of the decree is given over to a very detailed explanation of how the seminaries were to be financed and supported—the emphasis was on administrative procedure rather than on the details of the program of training. There were sporadic attempts to implement this decree almost immediately. In 1564, Pope Pius IV organized a commission of cardinals to put it into effect, with the result that in the same year the Roman diocesan seminary was opened. Charles Borromeo, Archbishop of Milan, founded three seminaries in his archdiocese: one for the complete formation of priests; another, with a shorter period of training, for priests who would work in country districts; and a third, where priests could repair the deficiencies of their training.

Most of the early attempts to establish seminaries were short-lived. There was no previous tradition on which to build, faculties were generally lacking or poorly prepared, and in many areas there was a genuine disinterest in reform; for example, in France, the decrees of Trent were not officially promulgated until a half-century later, in 1615.

The diocesan seminary as we now know it originated in the religious revival that swept over France in the first half of the seventeenth century. Its major figures included Pierre de Bérulle, founder of the French Oratory; Charles de Condren; Adrien Bourdoise; John Eudes; Vincent de Paul, founder of the Congregation of the Mission; and Jean-Jacques Olier, founder of the Society of Saint-Sulpice. Vincent was the first to divide the younger from the older students in major and minor seminaries. However, even at his death in 1660, the seminaries of France had neither a fixed curriculum nor a determined length of time for their training. Up to the French Revolution, most of the clergy of France were trained either by the Vincentians or by the Sulpicians.

II

Diocesan seminaries in the United States have been modeled on those of France, partly because the first seminaries in this country were founded either by Sulpicians or Vincentians.[11] Historic St. Mary's Seminary, Baltimore, the mother seminary of the United States, founded by the Sulpicians in 1791, is perhaps the best known example. Another reason was the vast number of émigré priests who fled the convulsions and anti-religious legislation of the Revolution and who helped spread the mentality of the French Counter-reformation in American Catholicism.

This situation was not altered but augmented by the great Irish immigration after 1830, since Ireland too had been strongly influenced by French religious movements. During penal times, the majority of the Irish clergy had been educated in France, in special colleges such as those of Douay, Lille, Toulouse, and especially Paris. The first Irish seminary, Maynooth, founded in 1795 when the Revolution destroyed the Irish colleges in France, was established by men strongly under the French influence. All Hallow's, founded in 1842 for the purpose of training clergy to minister to the Irish diaspora, was organized in deliberate conformity to the Sulpician-Vincentian program, and later passed under the administration of the latter group. Since the Irish element was to predominate in the American Church, the ideas that influenced the Irish clergy were to have a profound effect in the United States.

Any understanding of the nature and mentality of American seminaries must take into account the world into which they were born, for seminaries, like all other institutions, are products of an historical process, inseparable from the religious, intellectual, social, and political milieux in which they developed. For this reason, it is necessary to examine in greater detail that age which religiously is called the Counter or Catholic Reformation, which politically is known as the Age of Absolutism, and which socially and culturally is known as the Baroque.

In the sixteenth century, the Catholic Church literally had to fight for its life. The incredible speed with which the teachings of the first two generations of reformers—Zwingli, Luther, Calvin, the English Protestants—spread throughout Europe offers some indication not only of the desperate situation to which the Church of Rome had been reduced, but also the extent to which its vitality had been sapped by the scandals and abuses of the previous three centuries: the medieval heresies, simony, episcopal absenteeism and pluralism, the Great Schism, Conciliarism, and the wasting influence of the Italian Renaissance.

Of necessity, the Catholic Reformation was defensive in nature. Though it had its militant and aggressive aspects— the missionary work of the Jesuits and the crusading foreign policies of the Habsburgs—it was in the main a movement which laid great stress on avoiding the mistakes which had caused the Reformation and on holding fast to what was left. This attitude, understandable in a way, has left the Church with a strong stamp of conservatism which defines orthodoxy not only as unchangeable doctrine, but also as an unchanging juridical and liturgical structure.

By way of illustration, one need only contrast the freedom allowed Cyril and Methodius in their evangelization of the Slavs with the conservative position adopted by Rome in the Chinese Rites controversy. The attitude of the Church

was polemical and anti-Protestant, hostile to creativity and
new ideas, strongly dependent on politics and civil rulers as
a means of protecting or spreading the faith.

The Catholic Reformation was also strongly isolationist.
The predominant feeling, not uncommon or even incorrect
in an age when literacy and common education were com-
paratively rare, was that the religion of the ordinary person
could be preserved only by keeping him from contact with
anything detrimental to his faith—and this often meant
from contact with anything that was different or original, or
even moderate. Defensive walls such as the Index were
erected, and others such as the Inquisition were fortified.

In reaction to the excessive individualism of the reformers
and the humanists, personal freedom and initiative became
suspect. The stress on the individual personality and the
dignity of the human being, the belief that a man should
have freedom to expand and develop his personality in all
ways—these were rejected as coming from a humanism
which was thought to have been the source of Protestant
errors. Freedom and individual religious experience could
too easily be associated with the early Luther, or worse, with
genuine extremists such as Münzer or John of Leyden.[12] It
was these experiences that helped the conservative element
of the Catholic Reformation, personified almost to carica-
ture by Gian Pietro Caraffa, to dominate the entire movement.[13]

Since Luther and the reformers had stressed the invisible
nature of the Church, Catholicism reacted by tending to
emphasize its juridical nature. Law and obedience became
dominant themes, though this emphasis had been growing

during the Middle Ages. Ignatius of Loyola made obedience the principal virtue of his society and carried his interpretation of it to a degree which seemed to border on the suppression of human nature as such—*perinde ac cadaver.* The will of the inferior must be identical with that of the superior. These emphases helped the Church to meet the needs of the times, but they have been the source of numerous difficulties, then and now.[14]

Seminaries were an integral part of this Catholic Reformation and, if some historians can be believed, the most important part.[15] It is interesting to note that while Trent laid great stress on the necessity of priestly formation, it also demanded that it should take place apart from the universities. The cleric in the seminary was to be distinct, both in training and in external appearance. Literary education seems to have been presupposed but not demanded, the emphasis being primarily pastoral. And the tone was clearly isolationist.

This isolationism was based in part on a distrust of human nature, particularly that of the adolescent. For, said Trent, youth is an age "that unless rightly trained, is inclined to follow after the pleasures of the world." Furthermore, the Council demanded that boys be admitted to the seminary even before adolescence, "before the habits of vice take possession of the whole man." Implicit here was the Latin belief that is to be found stated explicitly in later centuries, viz. that at a certain period of his life, a young man is morally unable to accept the rigors of chastity unless he has been separated from his normal environment.[16]

These tendencies were not confined to religion. It is quite

easy to look at the Catholic Reformation and the age in
which it took place and to criticize it as purely reactionary.
Actually, it was merely a manifestation in the religious
sphere of something which had been taking place in Europe
for more than a century. The Protestant Reformation and
the Catholic Reformation coincided with the growth and
development of the modern nation-state. Beginning in the
last half of the fifteenth century, Spain, France, and England had begun the process of transforming themselves from
feudal monarchies into absolute, centralized governments.
The process was continued throughout the sixteenth and
seventeenth centuries, to reach its acme in the age of Louis
XIV.

Generally speaking, the emerging nation-states laid great
emphasis on centralization of authority and internal uniformity. This latter was especially strong in Spain, the foremost champion of the Catholic Reformation. In its full
development, absolutism stressed the principle of heredity
or legitimacy and the absolute nature of the ruler's authority, for which he was answerable only to God. Subjects had
no voice in or concern for government, their role being
essentially passive. The citizen's duty was obedience, and he
had little or no recourse against the abuse of authority.
Rather, it was presupposed, both in civil and religious life,
that the only possible abuse of authority was on the part of
the disobedient subject. Rulers not only derived their authority directly from the deity, but were generally considered to be especially inspired in their exercise of it. Hence
they were above all criticism.[17]

This tendency reached its height in the France of Louis XIV. The exaltation of the royal person took the form of ritual acts that were almost blasphemous in their approximation of religious ceremony. Gone was the implicit constitutionalism of the Middle Ages when the king had been *primus inter pares* and subject to a higher power, even if it were merely the often-abused power of the medieval papacy. Only in England did there linger the concept that the king was subject to, not above or the source of, the law—a concept directly contradicted by James I in his famous summary of the divine right of kings, *a Deo Rex, a Rege lex*. Kingdoms were highly centralized bureaucracies. All decisions came from above, while lesser officials postponed business, deferred and then sent up the bureaucratic ladder even the most insignificant decisions. The rulers, for all their autocracy, were prisoners of their own concentration of authority. One thinks of Philip II, the prudent, spending long hours regulating and legislating in the most minute areas for all parts of his far-flung empire, or of Louis XIV spending a full workday on *le metier du roi*.

The age also saw a great outpouring in art and literature. It is now generally conceded that in the arts, the Baroque period deserves to be ranked as one of the truly rich periods in human history. Yet curiously enough, there is, even in the high artistry of the times, evidence that there was an unfortunate dichotomy in the Christian life. Baroque art, as used in the Church, in accord with the dictates of Trent, was supposed to engender an overpowering emotional and religious experience, assaulting all the senses and virtually carrying the faithful out of themselves to the contemplation of heavenly objects.[18] John Eudes, for example, stressed rich and elaborate ceremonies as a way of strengthening the faithful. Personal piety tended to become divorced from the liturgical actions taking place at the altar. Ceremonies became great court rituals, and understanding of the Mass or active participation in it was not considered essential to the fullness of the spiritual life.[19]

Art, music, and set formulae of spiritual exercises replaced the liturgy (which had long been growing remote) as the conditions of religious experience. Mental prayer was made according to long and complex schemata. It is not at all surprising that religious life could easily become dominated by legalism and formalism, for these too were characteristic of the Baroque.

The Baroque was, at least in its later manifestations, an artificial and formal age. In its habits and manners, spontaneity and freedom were suppressed, and from the ruler down, in every lesser Versailles of Europe, life followed a ritual and formula as neat and set as a formal garden, as detailed as a Watteau painting. Even the arts and language came under the rule of law as governments founded royal academies to set the standards and legislate the purity of their languages. The result was often suffocation. Literature came to share with the liturgy the idea that something need not be intelligible to be effective, so long as it followed convention. As a result, the literature of the Baroque decayed into the cultivated obscurity of Gongorism and préciosité, and the exuberant spontaneity of its art was exaggerated into the grotesqueries and flamboyance of the Rococo and the Churrigueresque. Manners became stilted and clothing and ornamentation flowery and ornamental. For whatever exceptions there may have been, the later Baroque and the *ancien régime* in general preferred form to content.

This was the world of Vincent de Paul and Jean-Jacques Olier. Their contemporaries were Philip II and Elizabeth I, James I and Charles I, Richelieu and Mazarin, Louis XIV and Bossuet. They were products of their times and cultures, and it does not detract from their stature, as saint or man, to place them in the broader picture. Rather, it enhances their greatness, for they understood their times and strove to find, with over-all success, the means that were most suitable and most effective for reviving the religious spirit of their age.

Both men merit special study, for they exercised tremendous influence on the religious life of the times and on the development of seminaries. There is a striking similarity between the thought of Olier and Vincent, but this is not surprising in view of the close relations between them and the fact that for a while Vincent was Olier's director. Vincent was perhaps the more revolutionary figure, searching for and finding new methods appropriate to contemporary needs.[20] He broke away from the rigid formalities which had kept nuns out of the active life, and he devised a religious constitution for his community of priests that was so novel that it encountered serious opposition both from civil and ecclesiastical authorities. His organization of charities, along with his involvement in other works, including seminaries, was equally original.

Yet there is much about the thought of both men that betrays their age. Vincent's concept of the religious life was strongly colored by what would now be called the "ghetto mentality." Priests, he felt, should be men of zeal and flaming charity, yet at the same time their contacts with the laity should be minimal and confined only to those things vitally necessary to their vocation. They should be completely divorced from all political and social questions. Olier did not go so far as to lay any specific prohibition on his seminarists in this regard, but he did consider an interest in news of the outside world as something evil.[21] Both men were suspicious of intellectualism and both loved to quote the same scriptural principle: *scientia inflat*. They felt that the education of a priest should be pragmatic and pastoral, confined solely to what was useful for his vocation and ministry. Vincent seems to have been somewhat more guilty of this than Olier, and it may explain why his seminaries failed to develop a genuine intellectual tradition.

"If you study for any other motive than that of piety," said Olier, "all your knowledge will serve only to make you more vain, more full of yourselves, more self-opinionated and attached to your own private judgment; in a word, the more learned you become, the drier will be your devotion. To be learned without being puffed up is a miracle: *scientia inflat*."[22]

Uniformity and conformity were two basic virtues in Vincent's spiritual teaching. He devoted a long conference to explaining the necessity of uniformity, and he had a deep distrust, rooted perhaps in his peasant background, of the man who was singular and whose thought took him down new paths. Warnings against novelty were a fundamental part of his spiritual admonitions. Olier seems to have shared this idea also. "He judged it to be of the last [sic] importance that in a community there should be one fixed principle and rule from which none should be allowed to deviate except for solid reasons; and he expressly prohibited those who were moved to follow another path, however excellent in itself, from making it matter of conversation with others, lest it should have the effect of inspiring distaste for the accustomed method."

Vincent was not a legalist or a centralist in the strict sense of the term. His rules and regulations, though heavily derivative from Ignatius, were for the most part sparse, not heavily detailed, and above all practical.[23] But he did keep a close eye on the government of all his organizations and reserved most important decisions for himself. One of the greatest resemblances he bore to Philip II and Louis XIV was in the great frequency of his letter writing, a task incumbent on all centralized governments.

In Vincent's organizational thought, the superior occupied the central place. He was never to be contradicted and his opinion was to be accepted without question. Like his contemporaries, Vincent saw the stamp of divinity in every decision and step taken by someone in authority, whether civil or religious. The duty of the subject was to obey, and while heavy responsibilities were placed on the shoulders

of those who commanded, the basic principle was that,
though the superior might be wrong in commanding, the
subject would never be wrong in obeying. Civil authorities
were to be obeyed with equal promptitude. For all Vincent's
marvelous work in the realm of charity, one will search his
writings in vain for a denunciation of the social and class
abuses of his time. He never condemned social injustice or
the inequities of the economic system. His concern was the
poor person, not the sickness of poverty. An almost perfect
summation of the Catholic Reformation attitude toward
obedience and authority has been given by Olier:

Obedience is the life of the children of the Church, the com-
pendium of all virtues, the assured way to heaven, an unfailing
means for ascertaining the will of God, a fortress into which the
devil has no access, one of the severest, but at the same time one
of the sweetest, of martyrdoms, seeing that it makes us perfectly
conformable to Jesus Christ. He who faithfully obeys the rule
is invulnerable; whereas he who lets himself follow his own
caprices lays himself open to the assaults of the enemy, and runs
great risk of falling.[24]

Both Olier and Vincent were devoted to the liturgy, but
their first concern was always the proper celebration of the
rites and mysteries of the Church. In fact, their concept of
liturgy seems to have been a rather legalistic one, a matter
of ceremonies. It was an external view of the liturgy, but
one that was no different from, and in many respects far
ahead of, contemporary thought.

These two men left their stamp on the religious life of
France in the seventeenth century, both influencing and
being influenced by it. They affected the entire French semi-

nary system and ultimately the Church in the United States. Because the Church in this country owes so much to that of France, it was inevitable that many of these characteristics should appear in the American diocesan seminary.

III

The American diocesan seminary, as we have said, is primarily a cultural, intellectual, and organizational transplant. It is not only European in its background and traditions, but its establishment in this country, from the very beginning, was usually by Europeans. Of all the aspects of the Catholic Church's life in this country, it is probably the one that for most of its history was least affected by the American environment.

In the last half of the nineteenth century, there was a growing movement within the American Church to modernize and, in a proper sense, to americanize seminaries. In 1883, the American bishops of the Third Plenary Council of Baltimore rejected a proposal to establish summer villas for their students in imitation of the European pattern. Bishop Bernard McQuaid of Rochester said of priestly formation that "there is no justifiable reason why Church authorities in America should be hampered by the customs and usages of older countries, where innovations are looked on in the light of sacrilege." The establishment of the Catholic University of America was a reflection of the efforts of enlightened bishops to raise the intellectual standards of American Catholicism. Their efforts received a setback when Leo XIII condemned Americanism, a congeries of misplaced emphases that were supposedly being taught by the American Church (1899). A more severe blow was Pius X's condemnation of Modernism in 1907. Though necessary as a defense against a dangerous set of errors, his condemnation had the unfortunate effects of suppressing freedom of debate and theological investigation with the result that intellectual development and originality were severely inhibited, and the best study seemed to be that found in the "safe" Roman manuals.[25] The reaction was especially strong in seminaries.

The most alien element in the American seminary was its fundamental organization. It was grounded in the European educational system, and so avoided the American division of high school and college. The seminary normally consisted of two divisions: the minor seminary, which embraced the four years of high school and the first two years of college; and the major seminary, which, with philosophy, inaugurated the studies which were specifically ecclesiastical. This was the traditional method, but it was foreign to the educational system which eventually grew up in this country. It is still the predominant form, though a more native division has been gaining in strength and popularity over the past decade. Structurally, therefore, the diocesan seminary remained outside the American culture.

(In most other ways, the seminary followed its European counterparts, making few adaptations and sometimes emphasizing the more negative features of the original.)

The American seminary has always been and basically still

is an isolated institution. The separatist tendencies of the Counter-reformation were heightened in the United States by the phenomenon of immigration and the anti-Modernist reaction. The Church in this country has been until our time a minority identified with recent immigrants, essentially of foreign (read: Roman) allegiance, sometimes suspected, and always distrusted. It took on a ghetto mentality both by force of external pressures and by choice. The faith of the immigrant was maintained by keeping him from harmful influences and by making the Church a rallying point for his minority feelings. Thus the isolationist direction of the Catholic Reformation was greatly intensified in the New World.

This isolation was first of all physical, for the majority of seminaries in this country were built in rural areas. Sometimes this was the result of frontier conditions, but more frequently it was based on the principle that for the seminarian to be free and to be able to give himself wholly to his vocation without distractions, he must be located at a distance from cities. The remoteness of seminaries was thought to be more conducive to study and piety, and little thought was given to the disadvantages of such isolation.[26]

Much worse was the intellectual separatism. The mores of the old country were retained in their entirety and intensified in the seminary by the delicate position of American Catholicism.[27] Secular reading matter was banned altogether or permitted only by way of exception—there are in this country today seminaries which prohibit all magazines and newspapers not published by Catholic presses. Perhaps the only notable deviation made by American seminaries was the failure, mentioned above, to adopt the "villa" concept that the seminarian should spend even his summer vacations under the rule of the seminary in a summer camp. But in all other areas, he was under the vigilant eye of the administration, with a minimum of contacts with the outside world.

Seminary intellectual life was anything but exciting.[28] Frequently, the besetting sin was not anti-intellectualism, but nonintellectualism, not a downright hostility toward mental improvement, but a vague apathy and indifference. Sometimes the attitude was condescending, encouraging or tolerating intellectual pursuits only insofar as they could immediately serve the active ministry. The emphasis was ordinarily on piety at the expense of studies.[29] Nevertheless, there were opportunities for the better student to develop himself, if he wished. The seminary curriculum, particularly in philosophy and theology, was conducive to logical thought and to the development of an ability to analyze and distinguish. Unfortunately, philosophy and theology tended to become such closed and intramural systems, particularly after the Modernist crisis, that for all their depth they were still very narrow.

One reason for this situation can be found in the very nature of the major-minor seminary structure mentioned above and now popularly called the 6–6 system. When the college curriculum is divided, it is inevitable that there be a lack of emphasis on it or on its importance in the entire program. In practice there was usually little difference in the minor seminary between the level of instruction in the high school and that in the first two years of college—the minor seminary was the equivalent of six years of high school. In the major seminary, the last two years of college were overshadowed by the theological curriculum and became something of a vestibule before the really important and "practical" studies.[30]

The theological curriculum itself was almost entirely of post-Reformation, polemical vintage. Its teaching was static and unimaginative, and many texts in the theological sciences remained standard for an incredible number of years, usually untouched by any but the most superficial revisions. In many crucial areas, such as the theology of non-Catholics, the application of the virtue of justice to modern business life, apologetics, new movements in theology and exegesis, the American seminary remained staunchly backward.

Adding to this ineffectiveness was the fact that the overall program contained no provision for practical implementation of the material while it was being learned. The seminary in the United States never devised any practical form of internship (or vicarage, as it is known in some Protestant seminaries) to give the seminarian a time of supervised pastoral activity before his ordination. Advancement to the priesthood meant an immediate jump from classroom theory to parochial reality.

American seminaries were not only apart from the American scene, they were not even an integral part of the Catholic educational order. There was no coordination between them and the American Catholic universities and secondary schools. Being a world unto themselves, confident in their possession of truth, feeling little or no kinship with the lay college, the seminary usually ignored such matters as accreditation or new teaching methods. It remained satisfied with the system as it had been handed down, and saw no need to follow developments outside the seminary field itself. It was like a small island, watching the mainstream of intellectual and cultural life flow by. And, finally, this isolation extended even to relations with other seminaries. There has been little communication between seminaries, with a resulting confusion as to scholastic standards, admission and dismissal policies, curriculum, and many other phases of seminary life. Significant advances in one seminary may be counterbalanced by reaction in another.

Seminary life and discipline left little or nothing to the individual. It was highly regimented and adhered closely to the communal life, so closely as to prompt a frequent criticism that students were being prepared to be monks rather than parish priests. All important actions of the day were performed in common. As one seminary administrator has observed, daily routine was founded on the presumption that all seminarians get hungry at the same time, get sleepy at the same time, and feel like praying and studying at the same time.[31] The schedule of spiritual exercises was rarely drawn up on the basis of what the parish priest would be doing after ordination. Docility to the order of the day became a fundamental principle, and an almost superstitious importance was attached to "getting in" spiritual exercises. The principle that the bell was the voice of God displaced any emphasis on personal, religious experience. The seminarian did not guide or form his own life. He was trained, but not to make critical evaluations or decisions on his own. And at ordination he passed directly from this environment into that of the parish without the benefit of any transitional phase.

The action of the Council of Trent in founding seminaries constituted a complete break with centuries of practice that preceded it. The Council found in seminaries a solution to the most crucial problem of Church history, for no one can deny that the ages following Trent have seen a far higher quality of priest than those preceding. But, ironically, one of the most revolutionary innovations in the history of the Catholic Church has grown into one of its most static and ossified institutions.

3

Canonical Organization

To understand the contemporary seminary, it is necessary to know something of its organization and structure. Unlike other schools or corporations, seminaries do not usually have charters which detail the method of operation and specify the duties of all the officers in the organization. The organizational structure of seminaries is determined in broad outline by the Canon Law of the Church, but this foundation has been overlayed with numerous decrees and letters of the popes, the Sacred Congregation of Seminaries and Universities, and other congregations of the Roman Curia. Consequently, it is impossible to find in any one place a determination of what a seminary is, considered precisely as a juridical and canonical structure. It is necessary to search through a variety of official documents and even these in the end betray a curiously uneven picture, compounded of minute directives and broad norms, rather than a well-defined picture of offices, duties, and methods.[1]

A basic law of the Church is that "every diocese should

have, in a suitable place chosen by the bishop, a seminary, that is, a college where, according to the resources and extent of the diocese, a certain number of young men are trained for the clerical state." Larger dioceses are to have two seminaries, a major and a minor, though their exact nature is not defined in the law. Should dioceses be too small to support their own seminaries, or should those already established be inadequate, the bishop is to send his students to another diocesan seminary, unless a regional or interdiocesan seminary has already been established and is convenient. This latter type of seminary is frequently encouraged in Roman documents, and bishops are urged to be generous in support of them, "for there are many dioceses that cannot support a seminary of their own."[2]

Canon Law places the primary responsibility for the government and direction of the diocesan seminary on the bishop. He is to make all regulations for the administration, government, and advancement of the seminary and to see that they are observed. He should personally visit the seminary frequently, and seek to acquire a personal knowledge of the students. In all things, he is to watch over their training carefully. Each seminary is to have its own set of rules, both for students and faculty, and these are to be approved by him.[3] Even the fulfillment of the exercises of piety required by the common law are his obligation, for as the law states:

The bishop is to see to it that the students: 1) every day say morning and evening prayers in common, spend some time in mental prayer, attend Mass; 2) confess at least once a week;

receive Communion frequently, with due devotion; 3) on Sundays and feast days, attend Solemn Mass and Vespers, serve at the altar and practice sacred ceremonies, especially in the cathedral if in the judgment of the bishop this can be done without harm to discipline and studies; 4) every year, make the spiritual exercises for several days continuously; 5) at least once a week, hear a spiritual instruction closing with a pious exhortation.[4]

The bishop is to be assisted by two boards of governors, one of which is in charge of discipline, the other temporal administration. Each board is to consist of two priests chosen by the bishop with the advice of his consultors, though certain priests, such as the vicar general, priests who live with the bishop, the rector and treasurer of the seminary, and the ordinary confessors, are excluded from this service. In matters of importance, of which no specific examples are given in law, the bishop must consult these boards.[5]

Under the bishop, the administration of the seminary is to be in the hands of a rector for discipline, teachers for instruction, a treasurer (someone other than the rector) for financial affairs, at least two ordinary confessors, and a spiritual director. The code envisions the possibility that the bishop himself might act as rector, in which case he must appoint a pro-rector to act for him. A circular letter of the Sacred Congregation of Seminaries and Universities to the Bishops of Portugal also requires a vice-rector and prefects to help in the discipline, but it is interesting to note that, outside of seminaries for regular clergy, the law of the Church does not provide for an office of disciplinary dean.

This is the responsibility of the rector. However, custom and the size of most American seminaries have required the appointment of a special dean for discipline as well as a dean for studies.[6]

It is the duty of the rector and others in the seminary administration to insure that the students exactly observe the rules approved by the bishop, that they follow the prescribed courses of study, and that they acquire the true spirit of the Church. To this end the administrators should frequently instruct their charges in the rules of true Christian courtesy, as well as give them good example. The administrators are also to exhort the seminarians always to take reasonable care of their health, to attend to cleanliness of apparel and person, and in their relations with others to cultivate a certain affability together with gentlemanliness and gravity. The officers of administration are also to see that the faculty fulfills its functions correctly. Because of the seriousness of their responsibilities, the rector, spiritual director, confessors, and teachers should be priests who are outstanding not only for learning, but also for virtue and prudence, so that they may be able to help the students both by word and example.[7]

Within the limits set by the law, the rector is to determine the external exercises of piety and to establish "all those things which conduce to piety and every virtue," having taken counsel with the spiritual director. He is not to hear the confessions of his students except in particular cases and for grave reasons, nor can he demand an interior manifestation of conscience. The most important duty of the rector is to ascertain the fitness of candidates for orders and to transmit this information to the bishop. Though it is expected that he will seek advice and information from his faculty, as well as from all other useful sources, the responsibility for the final estimation of a candidate's fitness belongs to him, and it is he who makes the formal recommendation to the bishop in the name of the seminary.[8]

The spiritual director, in the eyes of the law, should be a person of blameless morals and great prudence, "a person who is both competent and a specialist in spiritual subjects as the other professors are in theirs." He should possess all the priestly virtucs, also have a comprehensive knowledge of ascetical and dogmatic theology, as well as a sufficient understanding of modern psychology and the behavioral sciences insofar as these are necessary and useful for his task. Because of the magnitude of this task, and because he is required to devote all his time to the spiritual direction of his students, he is never, for any reason whatsoever, to interfere with the external discipline of the seminary, nor should he be involved in any task that is incompatible with his primary duty. Authors commonly permit him to teach some classes, such as ascetical theology, catechetics, or sacred eloquence, but only for a few hours and provided that they are consonant with his office.[9]

It is the duty of the spiritual director to know the life and character of the seminarians so as to be able to give them prudent and safe advice regarding their vocation. This has two aspects, that of encouraging the fit to continue their studies and their advancement in virtue, and that of dissuading those whom he knows to be unfit, and in some cases of commanding them to cease their studies for the priesthood. He is also supposed to teach mental prayer in a special way, and from time to time to give them an appropriate meditation himself.[10]

The spiritual director is an ordinary confessor of the students, but the law of the Church also demands at least two other ordinary confessors to whom the students may freely go. If a seminary is under the direction of a religious order, the office of confessor may be exercised by faculty members, provided they have the faculties of the diocese and have been appointed to this office by the superior and bishop. Special appointment is required for an ordinary confessor of seminarians, and the mere fact of being a teacher in a seminary does not suffice. In seminaries operated by diocesan priests, the professors are permitted to be extraordinary confessors only. When there is a question of admitting any student to orders or of expelling him from the seminary, the advice of confessors or spiritual directors is never to be asked.[11]

The law of the Church does not go into great detail about the qualifications of faculty members, though it is stated that whenever possible they should have the proper degrees in their own fields. Individual regulations have been laid down for certain subjects, such as Scripture and Church history, but not for faculties in general.

Seminaries are to be used exclusively for the purpose for which they were founded, namely to train sacred ministers. Students who have no inclination to the priesthood are not

to be kept. Those who are admitted to the seminary must
be legitimate children, although subsequent legitimatiza-
tion by marriage suffices. They are to be of such dispositions
and good will as to give hope that they will serve permanently in the ministry. Before admission, they must
show testimonials of legitimate birth (parents' marriage
certificate), of baptism and confirmation, and of good
moral character. Those who have been dismissed from
other seminaries or from some religious institute are not to
be admitted until the bishop has asked of their former
superiors or other persons information regarding the dismissal; he is also to inquire of the character, dispositions,
and talents of the student, so that he may know for certain
that there is nothing in him that will be unbecoming to
the priestly state.[12]

The code specifies that troublemakers, incorrigible
youths, those who show a rebellious spirit, and those who
seem morally and psychologically unsuited to the ecclesiastical state should be dismissed from the seminary. The same
is true of those who make so little progress in studies that
there is no hope that they will ever acquire sufficient
learning. In particular, those who have committed any
fault against faith or morals should be dismissed immediately. Among those to be turned away from the seminary, Pope Pius XI included:

Whoever . . . looks to this state as a means to temporal and
earthly gains . . . whoever is intractable, unruly, or undisciplined,
has small taste for piety, is not industrious, and shows little zeal
for souls; whoever has a special tendency to sensuality and after

long trial has not proved he can conquer it; whoever has no apti-
tude for study and who will be unable to follow the prescribed
courses with due satisfaction . . .[13]

Later curial determinations have also specified cases of
mental disturbance and of sexual difficulties which are considered as counter-indications of a priestly vocation.[14]

Generally speaking, the legislation of the Church has
been insistent that the unfit should be turned away early in
their pursuit of a vocation, "at the threshold."

In these matters, hesitation and delay is a serious mistake and
may do serious harm. It is far better to dismiss an unfit student
in the early stages; but if, for any reason, such dismissal has been
delayed, the mistake should be corrected as soon as it is
known.[15]

For this reason, bishops and seminary rectors are obliged
to conduct a careful scrutiny and examination of the fitness
of candidates before their reception of orders. It is the duty
of the rector to gather such information from his faculty
and to present it to the bishop, who is also supposed to seek
a separate judgment from the rector. The diocesan board of
discipline is also to be consulted.[16]

The above summary is only a small sample of the general
legislation of the Church on the subject of seminary administration. Much of it is repetitious, and it is difficult to
find it in any one source, this primarily because such legislation has usually been prompted by individual cases or difficulties which arise, and it has an ad hoc flavor. Hence it
is difficult to synthesize the mind of the Church on this
particular point.

In some areas, Roman seminary legislation is too precise for an educational system which spans the entire world. Thus the decrees on the teaching of pedagogy, on the admission of seminarians who have been dismissed or who have withdrawn from another seminary, the triennial report which each seminary is supposed to send to the Sacred Congregation of Seminaries and Universities, all tend toward too great a centralization. Perhaps the most outstanding recent example was *Veterum Sapienta* which, though it did not deal with administration as such, imposed an impossible standard on seminaries throughout the world in regard to the teaching of Latin.

What is needed is a general plan of seminary administration which can be used throughout the Catholic world without the necessity of major adaptations and changes. Determinations for local or national seminaries should be left to the regional associations of bishops so that the seminary system in each country or region can be conditioned in the native culture and the native educational system. These latter determinations in turn should not be so precise as to destroy the autonomy that each bishop enjoys over his seminary, or so restrictive as to fail to account for local needs and variations from diocese to diocese.

In the present scheme of things, too much power is given to the rector. The cases in which he must consult his faculty or his dealings with them are for the most part unspecified. The regional associations of bishops, in legislating for seminaries in any nation, should take into account true decentralization within the seminary itself, and should include generic descriptions of the various offices and responsibilities within the seminary. This is particularly true in regard to admission to orders and dismissal.

A regional association of bishops would also be well advised if it were to establish some sort of grievance machinery or court of appeal both for faculty and seminarians. It is undeniable that injustices do occur, and that ordinarily a seminarian has no recourse but to change seminaries or dioceses—and it is even within the power of the rector to prevent this. There is need for some system whereby these cases can be fairly adjudicated.

4

Today's Seminarian

All too frequently, an element of determinism enters the thoughts of both seminarians and their superiors. Given the right set of circumstances, the proper changes of schedule and routine, the best available faculty, and more outside influences, the products of our seminaries will automatically be better. This is a naive but often unsaid and even unrecognized assumption.

A vocation to the priesthood demands a response on the part of the one called. It is something intrinsically spiritual and intensely personal. The nature of the response will be conditioned by the personality, habits, and background of the one responding, whether the encounter be on the road to Damascus, or in the reading of Romans, or in meditations in the desert. That is to say, the seminarian is the real variable in the seminary system, and it is vital that he be understood before consideration is given over to the improvement of the seminary itself.[1]

Almost all candidates for the priesthood at present were

born in the closing years of the Second World War, or in later years. This mere fact alone gives rise to an important sociological and psychological datum, unfortunately one that is by now a cliché, namely that their generation was not born under the sign of Virgo or Aries, but of the Atom Bomb. All their days have been overshadowed by the most frenzied search for peace and security that the world has ever known. Coupled to this is the fact that their parents are of the generation which grew up under the Great Depression and came to maturity under the war years, circumstances which have given rise to the attitude that their children shall not suffer the same disadvantages. This in itself has fostered an entirely different set of problems.

It is important to remember that today's young men are entering the seminary at the most crucial period of their development and maturation. The neophyte seminarian is at that stage of his growth in which he is trying to formulate for himself a sense of identity, molded by ideals which have been presented to him and modeled on those persons who have embodied these ideals for him. He is casting off the protective and guiding influence of the family and formulating an entirely new set of subject-authority relationships. He is growing conscious of himself as an independent person, and he feels a growing responsibility for his actions. In all of this he is frequently confused, his activities are disordered and apparently meaningless, and his awkward attempts to express himself and his newly found personality can easily be misunderstood.[2]

Even when all this is taken into consideration, it is dis-

concerting that one of the more notable features of present-
day seminarians is their apathy in the face of challenge. In
an age when challenges are of a cosmic and spatial dimension and when the indifferent collegian of the 1950s is
being replaced by a more active and involved generation,
it is perhaps too much to expect the ordinary youth to
respond zealously and energetically to the commonplace
routine of seminary life—but unhappily this is what the
modern seminarian must do. Admittedly, it is difficult for
anyone to find stimulation in the everyday activities of the
seminary, but it must not be forgotten that much of this
routine has its counterpart, for better or worse, in the life
of the parish priest. A common failure in the current generation is that they do not formulate a positive response to this
situation or find the courage to overcome the various minor
contradictions that life in the Church continually offers.
Immunized from many of the difficulties of life, protected
and sheltered, many young men find it difficult or impossible to face the discipline, rules, and enforced concentration demanded of them.

Generally, their response is either passive, consisting
more in withdrawal than reaction, or it may express itself
as hostility and criticism toward the seminary and its administration. This criticism and dissatisfaction astonishes
many parish priests who look back on the seminary with a
nostalgic, old-school affection. Their feelings go out to the
student who is apparently caught in a difficult and unsympathetic environment, and so they are tempted to blame
the seminary. It is undeniable that the fault lies as fre-

quently with the seminary as with the seminarian, but much of it does have its roots in the inadequate response of the individual.

One source of this apathy is a romanticized concept of the priesthood, based perhaps on an idealized view of life as a whole. This point of view sometimes gives rise to a questioning wonderment that a vocation cannot be achieved without self-denial—not the somewhat glamorous self-denial and self-discipline of the astronauts and Peace Corpsmen, nor the profitable self-discipline that prepares one for a lucrative and prestigious career—but rather the quiet daily application to a way of life that may offer little external reward. In short, they often want the priesthood on their own terms—a worthwhile vocation should be fairly comfortable, and, equally important, quick of attainment. What the incoming seminarian has encountered is nothing like the life of his priest-image—in fact, there is nothing comparable to it in modern American life except perhaps in military academies.

The sheltered life of many of today's young people presents a remarkable paradox, for it is a puzzling mixture of independence and dependence. No one can deny that the average young man who enters the seminary today is called on to give up a great deal more than his predecessor of twenty or thirty years ago. In our country today, the seminary is not the alternative to the ccc or war service for the average, talented young man. In following a vocation, a student may be giving up a quite comfortable life and one in which he has had a wide variety of goods and pleasures at his disposal. Like his companions, he may have had independence of movement, independence of social contacts (especially in dating), independence from burdensome restraints at home and from excessive work at school —freedom in everything except decision-making.

In our times, when such a high value is placed on security, the process of decision-making is frequently left to parents or superiors. In the seminary, their place is taken by rules, disciplinarians, and/or spiritual directors, with an over-all effect that can be deadly. And because the ultimate decision in a vocation belongs to the person called, many are unable to face it. Sometimes the realization of the significance of their decision overwhelms them within the first few days after entering the seminary. At other times, the act of deciding is deferred, and in extreme cases a student will adopt almost any tactic to force the seminary officials to make the final decision for him. Students in theology have been known to put off their acceptance of orders until they can have positive urging from their directors, or even from their psychiatrists!

This basic paradox often finds its expression in an excessive group dependence which is neither a social consciousness nor a manifestation of genuine altruism. Interpersonal relationships for some seminarians can be the expression not of the social nature of man and the Church, but of a hazy desire to be lost in numbers, a desire to feel accepted, to follow the group and to be saved the inevitable, heartbreaking day when they must stand alone, face to face with the reality of a vocation.

The students give themselves mutual support, but it is not the positive type that aids and helps the work of a priest; rather it is a negative one that offers abundant sympathy for "tension" and "pressures," often imaginary, almost always exaggerated. In its extreme form, this can be found, and has been found, in those students who postpone a decision on their own vocation in order to find out what their friends are going to do. Absurd, we can say, but it happens with distressing frequency. Such a situation is not only abnormal, but positively dangerous morally and psychologically.

One recent survey of Catholic college students summarizes this problem very well:

Another obstacle which sometimes seems insurmountable to the young is the moral cowardice which used to be called human respect and now is termed gang-pressure or peer-group influences. Certainly in his early years our [student] is unsure; his self-confidence wavers; he is extremely sensitive to the evaluation of his fellows; his fear of "not belonging" renders him vulnerable to the epithet, the wisecrack, and the snide remark. There is a strong impulse to drift with the crowd, sometimes for the sake of peace, at other times to reduce tension or merely to be accepted. He is badly in need, then, of that ascendency over the pressure of his peers and the spirit of conformism; of inner hardihood and resistance to the unreasonable press of the mob; of that personal autonomy which he likes to call freedom.[3]

One can easily see how these problems are magnified in the closed, all-male environment of the seminary in which the students not only live and work under close supervision and strict rules, but in constant contact and companionship with each other.

Compounding these difficulties are the standards of the modern world—standards of sex, success, failure, and of group relations. Every young man entering the seminary brings with him the outlook of the society in which he has been raised. In a society which stresses security, acceptance by one's social peers, which encourages early, frequent, and steady dating, and which exalts material success, the problems of the incoming seminarian are inevitably greater than in earlier years.

Unfortunately, many of these standards are entirely unrealistic, and a seminarian may see only the goal without facing the reality of the effort required to attain it. It has become something of a commonplace that at a certain stage in his seminary training, the student begins to dream of life on the outside—a special sort of dream, different from ordinary homesickness and discouragement. In his phantasies, he visualizes the type of suburban life which is today's ideal; perhaps he sees himself in the comfortable and secure life of the typical young executive, or, on the other end of the spectrum, as an Odyssian wanderer. Whatever form it takes, this sort of dream has a powerful fascination for a seminarian becalmed in the middle of his training. Normally, he overlooks the difficulties, sacrifices, and setbacks involved in any walk of life, because he is viewing life through a haze which is heightened by his isolation. Only the appealing aspects show through. Of course, this is not a problem peculiar to seminaries—it is to be found in other professional schools.

Certainly, there is no lack of idealism in today's aspirants to the priesthood. The point is that the greatest difficulty in our present society is not the *finding* of vocations, but the *keeping* of them. And this difficulty, as we shall discuss later, increases in direct proportion to the talents and ability of the individual student. Our modern seminarian has ideals, often very lofty ones, but for a variety of reasons he lacks the perseverance and strength to reduce them to practice for the sake of the Church. Thrown into a world which does not correspond to his concept of reality, he strives to revise the reality rather than the concept. The only alternative then is flight—the return to a more congenial environment.

It is obvious that in the context of the seminary mentality discussed in the second chapter, these tendencies are accentuated rather than eliminated. The isolation of the seminary tends to restrict the interests of the students and, together with the emphasis on perfection and self-knowledge, tends to turn his thoughts predominantly inward. Even while most zealously seeking virtue, he can become thoroughly self-centered. Socially, he is stunted by an exclusively masculine environment and by the lack of contact with others of his age who are in the process of solving the lay counterpart of the problems we have described, such as the subject-authority relationship, or the establishment of relationships preliminary to marriage. Even if allowance is made for the maturing effect of his spiritual formation, it must be admitted that, from a natural point of view, the seminarian's social and personality growth is definitely slowed. Constant, close, and sometimes abrasive contacts with the same people can produce a smallness and a jealousy that at times are abnormal in their intensity.

Fundamentally, a seminarian is challenged only as much as he wants to be. The schedule and routine of seminary life make it easy for a young man to drift. Unless he is confronted by very remarkable teachers and spiritual directors, he is liable not to meet any challenge at all, since his challenge must be basically interior. Unlike his counterpart in college or in professional training, the seminarian does not have the specter of his entire livelihood dependent on the works that he does in preparation. His challenge is sublime, but not nearly so immediate as that, say, of the medical or law student.[4] He must consciously make his own challenge, and it is the rare individual who can undertake this effort satisfactorily. The objective is clear, but the means of attaining it may be foggy and, in his mind, not at all essentially connected with the goal.

The duty of the seminary is to counteract these difficulties and to actualize the latent abilities and genuine idealism of the student. This endeavor is basically threefold. First, the seminary must provide the student, even before he enters, with a realistic and hardheaded view of what the priesthood really is. Second, the seminary must provide him leeway and encouragement in decision-making, so that he can genuinely guide his own life and evaluate men and events for himself. Third, the student must be given some means of identifying himself and his period of training with the goal of the priesthood.

5

The Faculty and the Environment

I

If the seminarian is the great variable in the process of training a priest, there is another, perhaps not as notable, but still worthy of special consideration. This is the seminary faculty member. At the lowest rung of the seminary structure stands the classroom instructor, normally a priest, though an increasing number of laymen are finding their way into seminary faculties. All of these are presumed to be competent in their fields and, in the case of accredited seminaries, holders of requisite degrees.

What type of man should be on the seminary faculty? The best summary has been given by Pope Pius XI in his encyclical *Ad Catholici Sacerdotii*, when he exhorted the bishops:

The seminary is and should be the apple of your eye, venerable brethren, who share with us the heavy weight of the government of the Church; it is, and should be, the chief object of your solicitude. Careful above all should be the choice of superiors and professors, and, in a most special manner, of the spiritual father, who has so delicate and so important a part in the nurture of the priestly spirit. Give the best of your clergy to your seminaries; do not fear to take them from other positions. These positions may seem of greater moment, but in reality their importance is not to be compared with that of the seminaries, which is capital and indispensable. Seek also from elsewhere, wherever you can find them, men really fitted for this noble task. Let them be such as teach priestly virtues rather by example than by words, men who are capable of imparting, together with learning, a solid, manly, and apostolic spirit.[1]

The seminary faculty member should be of the highest quality, spiritually and intellectually. He is literally a priest's priest, excelling even the generality of good priests in virtue and capacity for his task. Unfortunately, it is rare that the exact combination of desired qualities will be found in any one man. A man can be outstanding for his good example, his spirituality, his zeal, his pastoral abilities, and yet be totally unfit or even uninterested in the daily routine of seminary teaching. A man may be an outstanding teacher in some field, yet have little or no effect on the spiritual development of his students. The man who would fulfill the Pope's portrait of the ideal seminary faculty member is rather difficult to find in practice.

There is a certain degree of unavoidable conflict in the various aspects of being on a seminary faculty. A man can easily find himself torn between his scholarly and his pastoral instincts, and he can find that many things, ostensibly of great importance, intrude on his classroom preparation and teaching.[2] Thus it is of first importance that the faculty member shall have formulated for himself a hierarchy for all the tasks that he is given. Though the suggestion will arouse criticism, we nonetheless contend that for the ordinary faculty member the first and fundamental duty is to prepare and teach his classes as well as possible. Other things being equal, this type of person should be preferred over others when consideration is given to selecting a seminary faculty. Students are quick to notice discrepancies, and if a man fails in the basic task assigned to him, then only outstanding piety will redeem him. There will always be something lacking, something false in his approach to his special work.

In view of the importance that the Church attaches to the seminary faculty member, it is rather remarkable that there is no specifically professional training for men who will some day teach in seminaries. Though faculty members have graduate degrees, this fact does not differentiate them from teachers in any other school. The fact that they are priests is not per se enough to distinguish them from their brethren in the parishes. If the faculty member is a diocesan priest, he has usually been taken directly from the seminary, the parish, or graduate studies, to return to his alma mater. If he is a religious, he may have been sent immediately after ordination or completion of graduate study. In no case is there a professional preparation, or even a suggested program of study, directed at readying a man for the special task of seminary work.

It would seem feasible to initiate some such program, centered in one or two of the major American Catholic universities, a program which all those who are to teach in diocesan seminaries would be required to follow. A year's course could embrace some disciplines which would be obviously necessary, such as adolescent psychology or spiritual formation. But it could also include a thorough study of canonical and ecclesiastical legislation on seminaries, practical work under supervision in some seminary, and visitations of various seminaries in different parts of the country, including some Protestant and Jewish ones. Such a formation would not only bring an element of uniformity into the life of seminaries, but would also differentiate the work of the seminary priest from that of other priests and emphasize its unique quality.

Ideally, there is one quality that every seminary faculty member should possess, no matter what his professional preparation. This is the ability to establish a meaningful relationship with his students. If there is one word which sums up the newer approaches being used by seminaries toward their students, it is "relationship"—and yet it is nothing more than a reëmphasis on the teacher-disciple bond which characterized the training of priests in the early Church.

Relationship does not mean a permissive approach to students.[3] It is not a pampering relationship, nor is it incompatible with discipline. There is no place in seminary work for the attitude that every seminarian arrives trailing clouds of glory, that he needs only a few years of maturation and patience before developing into a fine priest. Anyone who has had even the most elementary contact with seminarians knows that the issue is far more complex.

A meaningful relationship definitely implies two concepts: communication and commanding integrity. By communication we mean that there should be a free and explicit interchange of ideas and feelings between the faculty member and his students. The seminary priest should be accessible to students, willing to listen to them, to encourage them to speak and live out their own ideals. He will try to understand each student and his personality, even when many aspects of it run directly counter to his own feelings. No matter how unfit a student may be, he has the right to a hearing by someone he can trust. An accessible faculty member does not try to impose his ideas on a student except in those cases where it is unavoidable or necessary, for example in dissuading the gravely unfit from going on to orders. Or, to put it another way, he does not take himself as the ideal and try to remold the student according to that ideal. Insofar as it is compatible with his obligations, he draws rather than drives the student to be worthy of the priesthood.

It is necessary to distinguish accessibility from proximity. The fact that a seminary priest is constantly with his students, for example if his quarters are located in the student section, or if he attends student recreations or participates in athletics with them, does not necessarily mean that he is either accessible or that his proximity is benefiting the students. As we shall later emphasize, he must have time to himself for his own personal development, else his influence on the seminarian is liable to be rather sterile.

One important part of this interchange of ideas and the one most ignored in practice is a certain receptivity on the

part of the seminary administration. Traditionally, the role
of the student has been entirely passive, and his place in
the administration of the seminary has been limited to
criticizing from the sidelines. Yet if there is to be genuine
communication within the seminary, the students should
feel that their constructive ideas and suggestions will merit
at least understanding and attention, if nothing else.[4]

This is a delicate question. It lays one open to the accusa-
tion of wanting to "let the students run the seminary."
There is a real danger that this can happen, and while such
a situation may please the students, it is ruinous to faculty
morale and thus a detriment rather than a help to priestly
development among the students. It is fatuous to think that
the students have either the maturity or experience to
dictate in any way the policies of a seminary. This situation
is particularly harmful when the students feel that they can
circumvent routine levels of administration in order to
make themselves heard on higher levels, for example to
go over the dean's head in securing permissions from the
rector, or in appealing for help to priests outside the seminary against some action on the part of the seminary authorities.[5]

"Commanding integrity" is a much deeper and subtler
concept.[6] Basically, it means that the student can find
actualized and personified in his teachers the qualities
which he is constantly urged to develop. This goes far
beyond the mere "good example" that administrators are
constantly urging their faculties to give: the "watch your
language or the students will be scandalized" injunction. It

definitely means that the faculty approaches its task and imposes its discipline on the students not because of administrative policy alone or because of a "party-line" attitude, but out of a deep conviction that this is the necessary and direct way of producing good priests.

On the part of the faculty, such initiative demands integrity. This will inevitably mean that there will be differences of opinion within the faculty itself, for men of deep conviction hardly ever think exactly alike. Necessarily, too, this will involve the faculty members in the dilemma of deciding whether to support administrative policies they do not entirely agree with—and of deciding how far this can be done within the limits of conscience and principle. But this demand does not deprive them of the right to make themselves heard. Disagreement with particular policies does not indicate disloyalty to archdiocese, bishop, or rector. It is a healthy sign of thought.

If communication is necessary between faculty and students, it is absolutely indispensable within the faculty itself. It is a *sine qua non* for effectiveness. Sometimes the members of the faculty become closed units who have no realization of what is being taught in other classes, or of how administrative decisions are being arrived at. Since seminary faculties rarely rival universities or even small colleges in size and number, there is no reason why the decision- and policy-making processes should not be a corporate action.[7]

While taking into consideration the law of the Church and the organizational structure of seminaries outlined above, both of which favor one-man rule, we must realize

that for a rector or a small tight knot of his staff to mo-
nopolize all the policy-making processes is a psychological
blunder of the first magnitude. This is equally true of the
bishop if he arbitrarily imposes policies on his seminary
without consulting the faculty. When the lower-echelon
faculty is reduced to the status of functionaries, the real
spirit will soon go out of the seminary, and that certain in-
tangible *élan* which makes the difference between life and
apathy is extinguished. What we shall say in Chapter 8
concerning obedience and authority in relation to the student applies *a priori* to the faculty and its relations with
higher authority. Many seminary administrators become so
concerned about the problems of their students that they
forget that nothing can be accomplished without a coopera-
tive and dedicated faculty.

Any man who embarks on a lifetime of serving in a seminary should realize fully that, for all its rewards, such a life is
often frustrating, boring, and burdensome. Because the gap
between theory and practice is often wide, the correspond-
ing feeling of insufficiency can be all the greater. Seminarians can be small, critical, indifferent, and consistently
ungrateful. If the teacher is a diocesan priest, the situation
can be aggravated by the fact that he has so little opportunity to do explicitly pastoral work.

Every seminary faculty member carries on much of his
apostolate by indirection. He hopes to make converts, to
help the sick and dying, to console the afflicted, through the
ministrations of the priests whom he is helping to form. His
day-to-day work is routine, and consolation only in the fact

that in the essential task of preparing priests, he is doing a work which no layman can do as well. It is a distinctive and unique work and requires extraordinary dedication.

For this reason, the faculty should have as much freedom as possible for self-development. There should be abundant opportunity for travel, for conventions, and for other contacts with those in his field, and for research and publication if such be his inclination. These are means that will help to maintain enthusiasm for his work and broaden his horizons and enable him to communicate to his students the benefits of his own experience and vision. It will help eliminate some of that parochialism which is the withering curse of so many seminaries.

II

Hans Küng was once asked: "Do you think that seminaries, under their present form of organization, are training priests to encounter the modern world in an appropiate way?" He answered:

No. By and large, seminary students live in a world that is intellectually and materially too closed. To be capable of proclaiming the Gospel to the world they ought to remain in touch with the world throughout their training. That is, in fact, what happens here at Tübingen. The seminarians, who have ordinary civilian status until they attain their subdiaconate, go to the same university as all the other students, since there are no separate theological faculties in Germany. Moreover, they are allowed to go and work six months or a year in some other university of their own choosing. In that case, they live with a family.

Asked what happens if the seminarian "takes a fancy to his host's daughter," Father Küng suggested that such a situation is better before ordination than after, and added: "In any case, experience has proved that our system is at least as good as the more restrictive systems."[8]

A similar, though not identical, situation can be found in some American dioceses. The Diocese of Winona, Minnesota, has established its college department of the diocesan seminary on the campus of St. Mary's College, a liberal arts school for men conducted by the Brothers of Christian Schools. The seminaries follow the prescribed courses leading to the bachelor of arts degree and attend classes with the lay students.

Likewise, no separation is made professedly between the college student and the seminarian in such activities as physical education, participation in extraclass academic events such as symposia and lectures, attendance at dramatic productions, and things of this kind. Seminarians take an active part in intramural athletic programs of the college . . .[9]

The seminarians have their own residence hall on campus under the direction of diocesan priests, most of whom are also faculty members at the college. They are under the direct supervision of the rector and have the required spiritual director, plus a number of other diocesan priests available for counseling.

Generally speaking, the authorities responsible for the Winona Plan have found it successful, and feel that it justifies any risks that may be involved.

The association with the college students in the classroom, at meetings, and in intramural sports helps students to mature. It gives them a more realistic appreciation of the hard facts of life: that success in the world demands ability, hard work, and many sacrifices, and is attended with much insecurity and uncertainty. This offsets somewhat the tendency to complacency to which seminarians living in a protected and separated environment are subject. Again, the association leads to lasting friendships with future parishioners, with an appreciation of the abilities, problems, and outlook of the layman.[10]

It is experiences and opinions such as these that bring one to the very heart of the present seminary problem, for is this not the trend that clerical education must now take? Is it not also possible that many of the issues that we have been discussing hitherto are endemic to seminaries as they are now constituted, and that they will be remedied only by the adoption of a new form of education which will combine the best elements of the seminary and the lay university?

This question has not been thoroughly discussed or studied in this country, but it is more than possible that it may become one of the more bitterly argued issues in the American Church within the next few decades. It is beyond the scope of this book to deal with the question as thoroughly as it deserves, but we should at least propose some brief thoughts for consideration.

First, it seems doubtful that the German system described by Father Küng is immediately practical for the United States without adaptation; or, to phrase it differently, it is doubtful that the United States is ready for such a system at this time. The Tübingen system, like the American, is the result of a complex historical development, but its line of development has no parallel in this country. Nevertheless, the American Church should study and evaluate the German system to see if it is applicable here in any helpful way, to ascertain if with modifications it could be the line of future development, and if it is truly superior to the present system.

Moreover, some sort of union between the seminary and the university should be the goal of future clerical education in this country. Though the Tübingen system cannot be imposed in its entirety on the American Church, it still seems that a gradual evolution to the seminary-with-university would be the best step that could be taken.

The ideal American seminary would be a school of philosophy and theology as an integral part of an American university. The students would have their own living quarters, as in the Winona Plan, since theirs is a distinct and specialized vocation having various common requirements, but they would attend all their classes at the university, where the theology and philosophy courses would be common to both clerical and lay students. In particular, theology and its allied sciences, such as Canon Law and Church history, should cease to be an exclusively clerical enclave. The life of the seminarians would be integrated as closely as possible with that of the other students, with the exception of those matters which are so explicitly clerical that they would serve no purpose in being common.

Such a union would be beneficial not just for the seminary, but also for the study of theology itself. It is a sad fact that most American Catholic universities and colleges do not have any real schools of theology, with the result that they can be distinguished from their non-Catholic equivalents only by a certain number of prescribed religion courses and by the presence of priests or religious on their faculties. Religion is often the least important discipline in a Catholic college or university, and it is frequently among the worst taught. Certainly, there is very little original work in theology being done in our Catholic universities, and equally little coming from the seminaries.

Most important, such an arrangement would provide a more normal atmosphere for the students' development, and perhaps prevent that regression which we shall discuss in our chapter on obedience and authority. The seminarian's personality development would then more closely parallel that of his lay counterpart. He would also develop a deeper understanding of the problems of the layman, and learn by experience that not all problems can be solved by simple syllogisms drawn from the standard manuals. He would play a more active role in his society and, it is hoped, be more a part of it than many clergy have been up to now. Such a union of seminary and university would break down that isolation which has been an integral part of seminary life up to the present. There would be more room for social and intellectual development, more challenges, more dangers (which, after all, are a part of life), and more tests for his vocation. It would provide competition. It would help to dissolve the small clerical ghetto which has so frequently grown up within the larger Catholic ghetto.

As we shall note later, very few seminaries have any real intellectual tradition. To develop one would not only cost a great deal, but it would take valuable time, perhaps generations. But a tradition, for all its imperfections, lies ready-made in some form in most of our colleges and universities. The student would find at his disposal a far greater variety of courses to take and minds to associate with than he ever could in the seminary as now constituted.

This arrangement would also permit greater flexibility in student schedules. In the present arrangement, it is almost impossible to meet all the demands currently being made of the seminary. Each time a suggestion is made for something new to be added to the seminary course of studies or for some new emphasis on a previously neglected field, seminary administrators answer with the very valid objection that they cannot possibly fit all these programs into an already overcrowded schedule. And overcrowded they are. Problems of scheduling, faculty members and their qualifications, and student class-loads all prevent the formation of an ideal seminary curriculum. The seminary-university arrangement would obviate these difficulties by its more flexible scheduling, and by its sectioning and frequent repetition of the same courses. And since no two seminarians have the same interests, and since there is no intrinsic reason why all seminarians must follow an identical curriculum, the seminarians would be free to adapt their programs to their own special interests and abilities or to the special needs of their dioceses.

For such a system to be successful, it is necessary that the university itself be willing to recognize the clerical segment of its training program as an integral part of the life of the whole institution. Otherwise, the entire movement would be doomed to failure from the start, and there might arise a situation similar to that presently found in the Catholic University of America. Catholic University, an ideal center for this type of training, is now surrounded by small seminaries which are every bit as marginal as those isolated in the smallest rural diocese. Most of the religious communities which train their students in Washington cannot afford to send them full-time to the university. It is cheaper to duplicate facilities.

There is a final factor to be discussed, namely the social environment that would be found in a coeducational university. More specifically, it is time for seminary administrators to make a serious study of the sexual environment in seminaries, and to ask themselves if the present isolationism is doing more harm than good. For many, it will be a matter of forcing themselves to face the fact that there is any problem at all.[11]

It happens frequently that a seminarian spends the years from his fourteenth to his twenty-fifth birthday almost exclusively in male company. Whatever else can be said of such social bifurcation, it is certainly constricting from a social point of view. While it has the advantage of protecting him from the "wiles" of the opposite sex and from external sources of temptation, it may also prevent his ever forming a normal and intelligent relationship with women. It cannot be denied that many priests approach the apostolate to women with a certain degree of fear—sometimes disguised as a forbidding coldness or uneasiness—which makes it impossible for them to give adequate direction; or, on the other hand, they may compensate by a too great familiarity.

This leads logically to the greatest objection to the seminary-university plan, namely that it will cause the loss of vocations. Many men in seminary work are convinced that to bring any normal seminarian into contact with women is automatically to jeopardize or destroy his vocation. This argument cannot be dismissed arbitrarily, because there is always enough evidence to support it in fact as well as in theory. It is not an imaginary danger. Thus, the problem is fundamentally a question of two conflicting views of the best method of preparing the priest. The one would isolate him until he is strong enough in his vocation to withstand sexual temptations after ordination. According to this view, clerical celibacy is not a normal or ordinary way of life and so cannot be prepared for in the conventional way. The ordinary activities and associations of university life may be a good preparation for persons planning to marry, but they are hardly suitable for those entering the celibate life. Rather, they contribute to worldliness, and may force the future priest into the impossible position of trying to reconcile two conflicting ways of life.

The opposing point of view is that such a situation tests a student's vocation far better than the tests of isolated seminary life. This view is usually summarized as "better that he leave before ordination than after"—a statement that is often made in its over-simplified sense. The true emphasis is on the fact that the priestly vocation actually emerges stronger, and again evidence can be cited, such as the Winona Plan and the Tübingen system, to show that this is true.

The question, finally, resolves itself thus: is the normal atmosphere and development that the seminarian would enjoy under the seminary-university system sufficient to offset the dangers to his vocation? In our opinion, they are. There can be, it might be pointed out, as much danger for the student within the confining walls of the seminary as without. Yet a seminarian so confined can easily develop a naive and ingenuous attitude toward women, or a deep-seated distrust and suspicion that is as detrimental to his moral and psychological growth as is too much contact. Reality itself, merely by having it around one, can often do more to strengthen a student than all possible spiritual direction, for it can lessen the danger of passive personalities, of deviation, of loss of vocation because of romantic phantasies about the married life, and the seminarian's attitude toward life and authority can grow at a more normal rate.

The greatest danger in such a system would come from the seminary administrators themselves. Their temptation would be to try to isolate the student within the university, to surround him with walls of rules and regulations, limiting his activities and creating a small ingrown cell within the school. In other words, they would try to re-create the present seminary environment in a different location. Hence there is need not just for a seminary structure, but for an entirely new mentality.

A lesser danger would be the loss of the distinct nature of

seminary training, this by returning seminary training so much to the mainstream of contemporary life that there would be the risk of making it little different from business administration or some other major field in collegiate life. To reach too far back beyond Trent is to ignore the painful lessons of a thousand years of Church history. It is absolutely undeniable that the clerical life is a distinct and separate vocation, and that its training must follow specialized lines. But since it is a preparation for ministering to the society that we now know, it must be a part of it, not some bizarre parallel of it. The correct proportioning of these two demands is the greatest challenge faced by seminaries today.

One important obstacle, perhaps the final test, to any substantial change in the seminary system at the present time is the financial one. Many if not most dioceses have invested heavily in large and well-equipped seminary plants, an investment that in some dioceses has run into the millions of dollars. These are specialized schools whose physical structures cannot easily be turned to other uses. Having invested so much in money, time, and men, few bishops will be willing to turn their backs on these seminaries in order to experiment with new and untried systems.

But obviously some sort of moratorium must be declared on the continued proliferation of seminaries in this country. There are too many of them to begin with, and therefore there is a needless reduplication of facilities. It is neither necessary nor desirable that each diocese have its own seminary. All too frequently, such a procedure means small student bodies, small faculties which are often ill-trained or inadequately equipped, small physical plants with inadequate libraries and teaching aids. The only advantage to be found in this type of arrangement is the close teacher-student relationship that at times becomes almost tutorial.

Even where facilities are adequate, there can be needless reduplication. In one large metropolitan area on the Eastern seaboard, there are three different dioceses each supporting its own seminary system. There is no reason why these three dioceses could not have combined their resources and established one seminary system which, with the tremendous resources available, could have been outstanding.

This leads to a suggestion which might be either a halfway step in the return of the seminary to the university, or else an alternative if total return is not practical. It is to reduce the number of diocesan seminaries in this country and to consolidate the training of priests in a number of high quality regional seminaries. This could consist of a core seminary complete with qualified faculty and all the necessary instructional and physical facilities, surrounded by various diocesan houses of study. In these latter, the seminarians could be under the direction of their bishops and diocesan-priest deans. This could be done with those facilities which are already in existence—in some geographical areas it would mean little more than the construction of living quarters as houses of study. If done intelligently, it could bear some relation to the geographical distribution of vocations.

But it is still doubtful that this would be as open and challenging as it should be. It is true that the introduction of outside influences into the seminary, no matter how well done, is still an essentially artificial process. Into the controlled and sheltered environment is brought a controlled and filtered sample of experience. The ideal is still a system which is an integral part of modern American education.

6

Intellectual Standards and Curriculum

I

Perhaps no seminary legend has persisted longer than that
the intellectual life somehow interferes with or degrades the
spiritual life. The impetus given this theory by Vincent de
Paul and Jean-Jacques Olier, plus the entire historical development of seminaries, have contributed much to this
situation. And, of course, the immigrant and minority status
of the Church in the United States has helped to prevent
the growth of a real intellectual tradition.

One of the best brief summaries of the condition of
Catholic intellectualism has been given by Richard Hofstadter in his book, *Anti-Intellectualism in American Life:*

> The American Church, which contains more communicants
> than that of any country except Brazil and Italy, and is the
> richest and perhaps the best organized of the national divisions
> in the Church, lacks an intellectual culture. "In no western
> society," D.W. Brogan has remarked, "is the intellectual pres-
> tige of Catholicism lower than in the country where, in such
> respects as wealth, numbers, and strength of organization, it is
> so powerful."[1]

In searching out the reasons for this condition, Hofstadter notes:

> More than any other group, the Irish put their stamp on American Catholicism; consequently, the American Church absorbed little of the impressive scholarship of German Catholicism or the questioning intellectualism of the French Church, and much more of the harsh puritanism and fierce militancy of the Irish clergy.[2]

In view of what we have said previously about the influences on the Irish seminaries and the Irish clergy, it is easy to understand how American seminaries were heirs to a long tradition of anti- or nonintellectualism. And the American clergy, unchallenged for generations in their domination of the laity, have simply spread and encouraged this same movement among Catholics in all stations of life.

Regarding the intellectual tradition of many American seminaries, John Tracy Ellis has remarked:

> Is it not true that there are still too many seminaries where high intellectual achievement is passed over with scant recognition; where relatively little premium is placed on academic distinction, on the use of students' critical faculties, on the merit of that kind of independent inquiry and originality of approach that open and expand the mind; on the exceedingly important need for differentiation of program for superior students so that they may not be denied the challenge to which their God-given talents entitle them; or, where even so commonplace a matter as reading good books is not honored as the vital force that it can become in a student's spiritual and intellectual formation? Has there not been too often a failure to counterbalance the warning against the altogether real danger of intellectual pride with the equally real danger of intellectual sloth?[3]

By and large, the American clergy have failed in the realm of intellect. The danger that faces the American Church now is somewhat similar to the one which Lebreton discovered in the Church of the third century—a growing rift and lack of communication between the scholarly, intellectual community and the mass of ordinary Christians. But in our country, at this time, with the rapid advance of education and the growing sophistication of so many Catholics, the intellectual group is not going to be a minuscule elite, and it is not, as in the third century, going to consist of clergy. There are numerous disturbing signs that lay Catholic intellectuals have already moved far ahead of all but a minority of priests.[4]

American seminaries have no reputation whatever for scholarship. Though many rank high academically and are well received by accrediting agencies, the fact is that there is very little original thought coming from the diocesan seminaries of the United States. Research, even in the theological sciences, has no place in the typical seminary administration. If it is ever considered at all, it is certainly not considered "practical," and always it yields place to the insignificant activity that the average seminary teacher is daily called on to perform.

There is no denying that seminaries tend to relegate intellectual competence to a position decidedly overshadowed by spiritual perfection and pastoral abilities. There has been and still is a distressing tendency to compartmentalize life and divide it into neat sections, each tagged with its own rating. It is as though seminarians came built in layers, and were expected to strengthen the more important aspects of their person before taking care of such extraneous items as the intellect. Seminaries are guilty of encouraging their students to use their talents as well as possible, and then of denying them the opportunity to do so.[5]

Trent and the centuries that followed were most concerned with the pastoral training of priests, something that had been woefully neglected in the period preceding the Reformation.[6] Our times are different, and with the rapid growth of Catholic education, with the spread to the parochial level of the present ferment of ideas within the Church, with the increase in reading and studying by the laity, the "new generation" and those to come are going to demand a stronger intellectual orientation if the clergy are to remain the spiritual leaders of their people. At the very least, the laity is going to demand intellectual adaptability on the part of the priests. A misguided emphasis on spirituality is not going to solve these problems.

Our first principle must be that we are training men, and that these men are individuals, that they are unities. Everything that is done in the seminary must aim at one thing— producing this particular, individual priest. Only when we integrate our training and stop dividing one aspect of it from another will we ever abandon that patronizing attitude which demeans intellectual excellence by condescension. Any consideration of intellectual development will always be based on this principle: everything that contributes to the excellence of the individual man contributes to the excellence of the individual priest. That is the context within which this chapter must be read.

Granted the necessity for intellectual attainment by the priest, the next and obvious question is: how much? This is a particularly difficult problem which in the concrete causes much discussion, not to say argument, not only within the seminary faculty, but also between seminary teachers and parish clergy. Persons on the outside looking in frequently feel that higher seminary standards will produce scholars rather than good "human" priests. The heart, it is complained, is overlooked in favor of the mind, so that it would seem that the seminary has become so intent on demanding study habits and degrees that it fails to train men or drops out those who can do real pastoral work. Dedicated seminary men, on the other hand, frustrated in trying to improve an intellectually sterile environment, feel that most parish priests would prefer to replace quality with numbers.

We have already said that no student who is incapable of obtaining an accredited bachelor of arts degree should be permitted to enter theology. This thesis can be persuasively argued from authority, from the nature of the modern apostolate, and from the very nature of theological study.

The first principle is taken from the encyclical *Menti Nostrae* of Pius XII, and is simply that the education of the seminarian should at least not be inferior to that of the layman who takes comparable courses of study. The minimum of seminary attainment should be the minimum required for graduation from an accredited liberal arts college, Catholic or non-Catholic. Normally, in our society, this means the achieving of a bachelor's degree in some field.

The second principle is: there is a certain degree of

factual, habitual knowledge that a priest has to have and has to be able to use. His ministry—confessions, counseling, teaching, and preaching—demands this as a minimum. This basic attainment is intrinsic to the exercise of the priestly office. It is something which should be judged very easily in a student's theology courses: does he *know* enough to function adequately as a minister to today's people? The ability to get a bachelor's degree would be *prima facie* evidence of this capability.

Third, if a student is incapable of doing the work required for a bachelor's degree, by what miracle is he going to learn sufficient theology for his apostolate? The answer that comes from many quarters is that it does happen in practice —under-achievers in philosophy do manage to survive theology. If this does happen, then one part of the curriculum, be it philosophy or theology, is obviously inferior or wretchedly taught. The theology sequence of moral, dogma, and ascetical, plus the courses in Canon Law, Church history, and patristic literature, should certainly demand a high degree of intellectual competence.

For the purpose of determining whether the courses taken in the seminary are comparable to those taken by laymen in outside schools, the following criteria are probably the most accurate, at least for the college years.

Accreditation. Though the number of seminaries accredited by regional agencies such as the North Central and Middle States Associations is constantly growing, there is still opposition to the suggestion that this is a necessary and vital step.[7] Apologists for accreditation have effectively answered critics by pointing out the fact that has so deeply impressed anyone who has ever gone through the accrediting process. The most important step in accreditation is self-evaluation and the self-survey that the educational institution is obliged to undertake. Self-knowledge is no less valuable for institutions than for individuals. When a seminary is forced to examine and justify not only the courses it teaches, but its very purpose and reason for being, it may frequently find that it has been operating principally on tradition and custom. The mere act of defining and justifying objectives can prove to be a shattering experience. Equally important is the fact of acceptance. Attendance at and graduation from properly accredited institutions of higher learning is a normal and natural part of modern American life. For seminaries to remain outside this trend is useless. Whether one likes the fact or not, modern education is judged by these standards, and the seminary will ignore them at its own risk. On the other hand, acceptance by these associations does indicate that the seminary has met at least the minimum standards of most modern American colleges and universities.

Entrance and Progress Tests. If seminary education is to be at least the equal of that in the colleges and universities, then it should have some very definite entrance requirements. Many seminaries now demand the American College Testing Program or something similar. Certainly, it is indifference beyond justification not to require something by way of entrance standards. One critic has said that such tests may turn away from the priesthood students who are capable of good pastoral work, but who lack the ability to pass these examinations.[8] Actually, however, a good program of entrance examinations will save diocesan money by turning away those who are incapable of persevering, and it will save the morale of both seminarians and faculty by preventing the influx of students who will depress the standards of the seminary or who will add to its dropout rate. Tests such as the Sequential Test of Educational Progress (STEP) or the Graduate Record Examination would also be very helpful in determining a correlation between seminary education and that of other institutions.

Follow-up Studies on Lay Alumni. Most seminaries lose all contact with students who fail to continue on to the priesthood and, in some cases, even with those who are ordained. Many of the lay alumni of seminaries continue their education at Catholic and non-Catholic universities, and a study of the quality of work done by them would give the seminary a valuable basis for evaluating the effectiveness of its preparation.[10]

If the seminary does demand the bachelor's degree as a condition for entering theology, it is only logical and fair that it should offer other fields of undergraduate concentration than scholastic philosophy. Any comparison would show that the mean achievement of seminarians in scholastic philosophy (as illustrated, for example, by the Graduate Record Examination) is inferior to that of laymen majoring in philosophy at Catholic universities. The obvious reason is that all seminarians are compelled to major in philosophy, despite their personal preferences or abilities.[11]

But obviously not all students, even of bachelor caliber, are able so to concentrate on philosophy as to make a major field of it. To demand it as the only major is also to deprive the Church of many other skills and fields of concentration that the students would choose. Once again, the advantages of reuniting the seminary and the university are apparent, for very few seminaries have the facilities to offer more than one or two majors.

Steps such as these would greatly aid in the standardization of seminaries. It has already been stressed that seminaries in the United States grew up in isolation from one another, with the consequence of variations in areas such as entrance requirements, disciplinary approaches, minimum scholastic achievement, and the like. These variations are most obvious in the fields of curriculum, scholastic standards, and the minimum attainment required for ordination.

For this reason, one of the most desperate needs of the American seminary is some sort of cohesion. Since the seminary will never be better than what the bishops want, it is desirable that the bishops of this country approach the question on a national level. Our seminaries need a thorough and painstaking evaluation, similar to that made of universities and medical schools by Abraham Flexner and that made of high schools and teacher preparation by James B. Conant, or that made of Protestant seminaries by Richard Niebuhr, Daniel Williams, and James Gustafson.[11]

Such an investigation could formulate some sort of core curriculum, perhaps even a much needed revision of the entire theology sequence, basic disciplinary demands, and

minimum attainment for studies. These basic standards
would then be demanded of all American seminaries. Such
an evaluation would be one of the greatest single steps forward that the American Church could take. Though there
are many ways in which such a survey could be made, the
following outline, for the sake of example and as a concrete
suggestion, will serve as an illustration of how it could be
carried out.

The regional association of American bishops could appoint a committee responsible for drawing up a report on
the training of priests in the United States, the Bishops'
Committee for Seminaries. It would consist of one American bishop as president, and under him a chairman who
would be responsible for most of the routine work of the
committee. The membership would consist of ten men:
five seminary priests (administrators or teachers), chosen
from among diocesan priests and religious who are involved
in the training of diocesan priests. These should be men
outstanding in their fields. The other five members would
be chosen from among men who are involved in Catholic
education other than in seminaries, of whom at least three
should be laymen—if all five were responsible and outstanding laymen, it would be ideal.

The Committee on Seminaries would be responsible for
choosing a Field Committee which would be composed of
the men who would do the actual survey. This would consist of three men involved in seminary work: one would deal
with all matters of administration and curriculum, one
would deal with spiritual and counseling programs, and the

third would be concerned with student life and discipline in each of the seminaries surveyed.

The Committee on Seminaries would also appoint as consultors three men outstanding in the field of Protestant seminary education, preferably from among those involved in the 1957 survey of Protestant theological schools. They would be invaluable in suggesting methods for procedure, and in those areas where the problems are common.

The actual procedure could be as follows:

1. The Field Committee would draw up a questionnaire, to be approved by the Committee on Seminaries, after which it would be sent to all diocesan seminaries in the United States, and to all abbeys, monasteries, and religious houses involved in the training of diocesan priests, and to be answered within three months.

2. The results would be collated by the Field Committee and again submitted to the Committee on Seminaries. Out of this, the program for the field visitations would be drawn up.

3. The Field Committee would make a visitation of all the aforementioned seminaries for the purpose of evaluating them in every possible way. If necessary, a second field committee would be appointed.

4. On the basis of this field survey, the Committee on Seminaries would draw up a full and final report on the training of Catholic priests in the United States, and make its recommendations to the regional association of bishops.

The matters that the committees could study are countless: the professional preparation, both academic and otherwise, of the seminary faculties; morale on seminary faculties; student-faculty ratios; entrance standards and qualifications of students; norms for student dismissals; academic standards; physical plants and the expenses involved; the degree of overbuilding in seminaries; the relations of the seminary to the local community, to the parochial clergy, to the diocesan curia, and to local lay colleges; the degree of centralized administration; academic freedom; the degree of isolation of the students; the specific aims and objectives of each seminary; all the various aspects of student life and discipline, including morale and relations with the faculty; the curriculum, particularly in theology; the character and personality of the modern student; the opinions of seminary training held by alumni, lay and clerical; the relative effectiveness of the present seminary as against the proposed seminary-university merger.

The recommendations of the Committee on Seminaries would have only the effect that the bishops would want to give them. In this respect, moral suasion and good example would be most important, since each seminary is only going to be as good as the ordinary of the place wants to make it. But a general improvement of seminary training and updating of the whole system would eventually bring into line not only the occasional recalcitrant, but also those seminaries which are conducted by religious for their own members. If the recommendations of the Committee on Seminaries were to be accepted, then the committee should be made a permanent body for the purpose of enforcing its recommendations.

This type of accreditation should not make the mistake of trying to prescribe in too great detail what each seminary should do. There are too many individual needs from one area of the country to another. Experience has shown that it is impossible to govern a widespread educational system from one central authority. However, the present disparity is appalling, and even an occasionally oppressive uniformity would be preferable.

Earlier, we proposed a system of reciprocity for American seminaries similar to that which is found in some other professional schools in this country.[18] Specifically, we suggested that the involuntary dropout from one seminary should not be allowed to be received into another, and that voluntary transfers should be rigidly governed, a suggestion that has since been severely criticized.

We strongly reiterate the suggestion here. It is a very common experience to see a student who is unable to survive scholastically in one seminary enter another and be graduated easily. Either one seminary is too difficult or the other is too lax, but this sort of situation definitely indicates that something is wrong. Seminarians can and do pass from one seminary to another without being required to present the obligatory letters of recommendation. In those seminaries to which benevolent bishops are wont to send their students, it is possible to find students who are "seminary hoppers," having been through two or three different seminaries. Often they are obvious misfits, but they can be ordained eventually if they keep trying. It is a commonplace among seminary authorities that if a man really wants to be ordained in the United States, no matter what his qualifications, he will eventually succeed in being ordained. There is always a *refugium peccatorum* and someone willing to exalt numbers over quality.

It will immediately be objected that the stringent requirements we propose would penalize many good students who for reasons beyond their control have done poorly in one seminary and wish to transfer to another. There would be obvious exceptions to reciprocity. Often students are too immature when they first enter the seminary and make impetuous decisions. Sometimes there are personal or family problems or personality clashes or just plain injustices on the part of the seminary staff.

If seminaries were more standardized, part of this situation would be remedied. Yet there would always have to be some kind of court or some mode of appeal to which the involuntary dropout could have recourse. Even though there might be some injustices in particular cases, a system of reciprocity would be vastly superior to the present haphazard and ill-organized method of operation. It would aid immeasurably in raising the standards of the clergy, it would hinder the unstable, it would deter the seminarian in a superior seminary from looking for an easier path to ordination, and finally it would discourage bishops from moving under-achievers or the incompetent from a high-standard institution to a lower one.

II

Probably no other aspect of higher education in this country has as many and conflicting demands made on its curriculum as does the seminary. From one point of view, the seminary is faced by more accreditors than any comparable institution. It is frequently criticized for not meeting all these demands and at the same time for not equalling all other schools in the number, variety, and depth of its offerings.

The first of the governing bodies that immediately influence the seminary curriculum is the Holy See, which has established the basic structure and the courses to be followed. But within the broad context of what Rome demands, the seminary may have to meet the demands of regional accrediting bodies, of state educational agencies, particularly in the case of junior college departments, of the bishops, of the particular traditions and practices of the religious community operating the seminary (if this be the case), and finally the demands of individual deans and rectors. In addition to all this, though extrinsic to it, are the demands of the educated laity who have their own ideas about what the future priest should be studying.

The basic curriculum of the seminary has been formulated by the Holy See, which has in some instances merely given a general outline of the course of studies and in others has been very specific even to the point of determining the number of class hours. Canon Law requires at least two years' study of rational philosophy according to the scholastic method, together with the study of kindred subjects, that is, of the vernacular, of Latin and Greek language and literature, of profane history, mathematics, and the natural sciences. The theology course, which is supposed to last at least four years, includes dogma, moral, Scripture, Church

history, Canon Law, liturgy, sacred eloquence, and ecclesiastical chant. There are also to be lectures in pastoral theology, and some formal attempt at the practical exercise of
what is learned theoretically.[13] Time and again, this basic
sequence of courses has been added to or expanded by other
pronouncements of Rome, whether by the pope directly or
through one of the Roman congregations.

The theological curriculum was settled in some detail by
the 1931 constitution, *Deus Scientiarum Dominus*. Because
of this decree, and because of the common tradition which
went into its formulation, the curriculum in theology generally tends to be more stable and more uniform from seminary to seminary than does that in philosophy or college.
Unfortunately, the quality of the theological training suffers
from some serious defects. There is an excess of compart-
mentalization and division, with frequent overlapping of
some material and total neglect of other areas. Dogma,
moral, ascetical theology, and Canon Law are often taught
as though they had no relation to each other. Moral theology frequently overlaps Canon Law, and it is quite possible that a single topic, such as the study of the virtues, can
be taught in ethics as well as in dogma, moral, and ascetical
theology. Similar repetitions can be found in biblical, patristic, and systematic theology. The theological manuals are
often less concerned with teaching principles or outlook
than with grinding out readymade answers and apologetic
refutations of long-dead errors, shooting, as the saying goes,
where the enemy was last seen. Biblical texts and quotations
from the Fathers are generally used only as polemical weap-

ons, and this frequently out of their original context. Historical development is usually overlooked in favor of the scholastic approach.

As we have mentioned before (see Chapter 2), this approach has its value, and in the hands of a discriminating teacher can be the means of giving a student valuable insights and abilities, particularly in analysis and distinction; but it can also lead to rote memorization. The manuals often reflect a system turned in on itself, and have little or no relation to theology as a way of life or as something to be proclaimed throughout the world. Their language is often dead not because it is Latin, but because of the mode of thought that lies behind it. The solutions to these deficiencies will not come easily; for example, the task of writing new texts embodying the latest developments in Scripture and dogma will take generations. In the meantime, seminaries must adapt as well as they can, while at the same time holding to what is best in the scholastic tradition.

By and large, it is the college curriculum of the seminary that is subject to the most criticism, because it is the one area that can be compared with some other existing form of education. Here again the Holy See has legislated, though the various directives are scattered among myriad decrees and instructions, so that it is difficult actually to ascertain what Church authority does want in the college program. Papal documents have generally stressed the need for humane and scientific studies. Rational philosophy, according to the code of Canon Law, is supposed to include the study of logic and the philosophy of language, ontology, psychol-

ogy, cosmology, theodicy, ethics, and the history of philosophy. The Sacred Consistorial Congregation, writing to the
Bishops of Italy, outlined a program that included mathematics, natural science, physical science, Italian (that is, the
vernacular), Latin and Greek literature, and secular history.[14] The Sacred Congregation of Seminaries and Universities, writing to the Bishops of Germany, stated that the
teaching of cosmology and rational psychology should be
accompanied and aided by courses in physics, chemistry,
and experimental psychology. Other documents have stressed
the importance of Latin, both as a discipline and as a means
of instruction, of Greek, of Gregorian Chant, and sacred
art.[15] A decree of the Sacred Congregation of Seminaries
and Universities of December 21, 1944, makes pedagogy a
required subject, and states that during the years of philosophy, it must be taught at least one hour a week for two
years.[16]

Using these as guidelines, we find that the basic curriculum of the college department should include:

> Logic
> Cosmology
> Ontology
> Psychology
> Theodicy
> Ethics
> History of Philosophy
> Experimental Psychology
> Physics
> Chemistry

English Literature
American Literature
Latin Literature
Biblical Greek and Greek Literature
European and/or American History
Speech
Mathematics
Gregorian Chant
Sacred Art

By a conservative calculation, this would total about one hundred hours of class out of the total needed for a bachelor's degree; and in actual practice it would probably be more.

With the exception of the over-emphasis on Latin and Greek, one cannot find much fault with this sequence of courses as the core of a good liberal arts education for a modern seminarian. Unfortunately, difficulties arise from the accrediting agencies and their various requirements, particularly that the curriculum be conformed to the stated purposes of the school. Thus, accreditors would find fault with the above for not including courses in sociology, economics, political science, modern philosophy, and modern foreign languages. The needs of individual dioceses must also be considered. A bishop who intends to use his priests to staff diocesan high schools would want heavier emphasis on teacher preparation, and in southwestern dioceses there is the pressing need for a thorough knowledge of Spanish. Demands such as these will expand and eventually overcrowd the curriculum.

Finally, there are the varying and often insistent recommendations of laymen who often feel that some important subject is being slighted. Philosophers want more philosophy, sociologists more sociology, historians more history, and so on. Daniel Callahan summed up this attitude when he said of the average seminarian that "unless he makes special efforts, it is more than likely that the graduate of a seminary will have only the barest acquaintance with literature, psychology, sociology, economics, history, and political science. He will almost surely not have wrestled directly with the thought of Hegel, Marx, Freud, Darwin, or Kant. . . ."[17]

From all this, certain conclusions can be drawn. First, it is basically impossible to legislate the curriculum of a worldwide educational system from one source. While it is right and proper that such authority should lay down the broad outlines of the seminary program of studies, this should be done in a way that is both easily accessible and ascertainable. Generally, more leeway should be given to the regional associations of bishops to adjust the course of studies to the needs of their areas and to special circumstances. Second, even granted this autonomy, it is still doubtful that many seminaries will have the faculties and resources to carry out the ambitious program that the above paragraphs suggest, or to compete with even small liberal arts colleges. What is needed is either a coalescing of seminaries with a consequent more efficient use of resources or, as already suggested, the union of seminary and lay university. Third, it is evident that it is neither desirable nor possible for a seminarian to become a true expert or even very well acquainted with all the fields that have been enumerated. What is needed is a greater variety of offerings and a greater flexibility in the courses taken by the individual students. Here again, we must fall back on one of the two possible solutions: fewer seminaries or integration of the seminary and the university.

The greatest difficulty facing the seminary in this context will be that of developing a genuine intellectual attitude. In many seminaries, this will mean the total reversal of many years of tradition, a violent shifting of gears to change emphasis and to restore the intellectual life to its proper perspective. In others, it will be something which, with all good will, will take generations of students for its accomplishment and, of course, it would be better accomplished by acting on the two proposals which have already been emphasized in this chapter.

However, even within the context of the present system, there are areas which are under the control of the faculty and which should be reformed. First, there is the lack of integration within the seminary curriculum and within individual faculties. Subjects are too often taught in isolation, as we have mentioned earlier, and there is little attempt to relate them to other fields or to present a synthesis of the whole. This is rather surprising in view of the supposed unanimity of goals and means that are to be found in seminaries. This difficulty could be remedied in part by the adoption of team teaching and by the use of coordinating seminars. A well planned annual required reading list would help toward the same goal. Most important, a real communication within the seminary faculty, genuine cooperation and willingness to work with others to teach a subject rather than an individual course, could produce a system of education in which the student would be able to relate his subjects to one another and to get a comprehensive view of what he is working toward.

Greater emphasis could also be laid on the behavioral sciences, for more and more in these days the priest is called on to be a counselor. One psychiatrist has estimated that seventy-five per cent of the people who seek psychiatric help see a clergyman before seeking more specifically professional advice. If this is even partly true, it places on the seminary a heavy obligation to see that the priests of the future are adequately prepared to recognize symptoms of mental disorder, that they understand thoroughly their own limitations in this area, and that they are skilled enough to guide their clients into the proper medical channels. Finally, those dioceses which assign their priests to the staffs of high schools should see that they are thoroughly grounded in adolescent psychology and counseling.

In addition to their immediately practical value, the study of such subjects as psychology, counseling techniques, sociology, and anthropology, aids greatly in the formation of intellectual adaptability and of broadness of outlook. Obviously, this is not merely an ability to master the professional jargon, but is a definite point of view which enables the priest better to understand his environment and the forces at work in his parish—whether it be urban or rural, inner city or suburban, wealthy or poor.

Further, the priest is a liturgist by reason of his ordination. The Second Vatican Council has declared liturgy a major subject in the seminary curriculum and an integrating force, giving coherence and unity to all the disparate subjects that the seminarian studies. As an integrating force in the curriculum, liturgy is better suited to the theological division than to the collegial. There is, however, in the college curriculum a subject which is close to the liturgy and which actually derives from it, one which is receiving renewed emphasis in the current ferment of ideas within the Church. This is homiletics.

Homiletics is in a deplorable condition if one can believe the current criticisms by the laity. It is undeniable that the preaching of the word of God has frequently been defective in the Church; this is partly a reaction to the sacramental character given to the word by the reformers, and the resulting Catholic tendency to stress the *ex opere operato* nature of the sacraments. This tendency is beginning to be arrested. Theologians, inspired perhaps by current Scripture studies, have begun to formulate a teaching on the word of God which is closer to what is found in Paul, the Psalms, and other parts of the Bible. Whereas earlier thought had viewed preaching merely as an external grace, more or less accidental to religious experience, contemporary thought reëmphasizes its sacramental character, its closeness to the Incarnate Word, Jesus Christ, and its importance in Christian growth. Scripture and the preaching of God's word are seen as vital and living, possessed of their own special efficacy. Homiletics is a proclamation of God's successive reve-

lation of himself through Scripture, so that to be ignorant
of Scripture, as Jerome said, is to be ignorant of Christ. To
be ignorant of the word clothed in human terms is to be
ignorant of the Word clothed with human nature. Thus,
the Second Vatican Council has closely tied preaching to
the liturgy, which itself is an expression of revelation.

The ministry of preaching is to be fulfilled with exactitude
and fidelity. The sermon, moreover, should draw its content
mainly from scriptural and liturgical sources, and its character
should be that of a proclamation of God's wonderful works in
the history of salavation, the mystery of Christ, ever made present and active within us, especially in the celebration of the
liturgy. . . .
By means of the homily, the mysteries of the faith and the
guiding principles of the Christian life are expounded from the
sacred text, during the course of the liturgical year; the homily,
therefore, is to be highly esteemed as part of the liturgy itself;
in fact, at those Masses which are celebrated with the assistance
of the people on Sundays and feasts of obligation, it should not
be omitted except for a serious reason.[18]

Undoubtedly, in this age of mass education and mass
communication, the laity tends to be much more critical of
preaching than in the past. Even the priest's style of delivery
is open to criticism and to comparison with the diction and
rhetoric of the mass media. The priest himself has a difficult task in homiletics. Public speaking is something that
comes naturally and easily to very few. Furthermore, he is
limited as to the amount of time at his disposal, and his
audience may vary according to background, education, and
preferences. Strangely enough, however, efforts to help the
future priest prepare for situations like these often meet the

most appalling indifference on the part of seminarians. Perhaps this is due to the lack of emphasis given to oral reading and speech preparation in primary and secondary schools today. But whatever the reason, before the status of preaching can be improved, the average seminarian must be convinced that his first purpose in the pulpit is to be heard and understood.

In many seminaries, the custom of having public reading during meals still prevails. Though it is an archaism and should be discontinued on social grounds, if no other, it does fulfill a vital function—it forces students to stand up in public and to read aloud. It is possible to encounter students in the later years of college who never in their lives have been before a group to read or give a talk, and who have never had their faults of speech, pronunciation, and diction pointed out to them. It would be well if every seminary devoted one full year of the speech program to voice training and development under the guidance of a trained technician, and another full year to interpretative reading. Some attention should also be given to the basic principles of audience psychology. Far from being visionary, this education would prove of great practical value, and would save much work and agony in the later years of theology.

Any discussion of seminary curriculum can be carried on indefinitely, for, as we have already mentioned, there is a wide variety of opinions as to what should be taught in the seminary. What we have said about the behavioral sciences and homiletics could just as easily be applied to any other subject. The result would be an expansion and crowding of the curriculum which would suffocate rather than aid the education of the seminarian. But we must repeat: what is needed is a situation in which the seminarian has the *opportunity* to pursue the subjects of his special interest or of his special need—and this is something which is extremely difficult, if not impossible, under the present seminary system.

7

Spiritual Formation

Several years ago a diocesan priest asked this writer: "What is wrong with our seminaries that our students don't seem to be learning what they should? They think that meditation and other spiritual exercises are something to be done in the seminary and forgotten after ordination." From habit, my first impulse was to absolve the seminary and place all the blame on the shallowness of the students. Unfortunately, the answer is not that simple. To find a reason for and solution to such a situation, it is necessary to take a long, critical look at the spiritual development program of the seminary, and to expunge those aspects of it which fail to give the student full opportunity for personal spiritual progress.

The law of the Church on spiritual exercises has already been quoted in chapter 3 (see pp. 57–58). It would be rash in the light of this canon and the Church's long experience to deny all utility to these exercises, and to demand that something entirely new be substituted. It is true that these exercises are drawn from the religious life, and that when

the first seminaries were founded, the spiritual formation
program was drawn from the only available source, the life
and rules of the religious orders and congregations. There is
at the present time a reëxamination taking place whose purpose is to try to move the spirituality of the diocesan priest
away from this religious orientation and toward a spirituality
which is more specifically priestly. This is sometimes called
"functional" spirituality, because it seeks the sanctification
of the priest in and through the exercise of his priestly office.
However, these concepts are not as yet well developed, and
means whereby they would be put into practice are not
clear. Further difficulties arise in trying to apply such an
approach to the seminary, since the seminarian is in a stage
of preparation for the priesthood, and does not have any
specific office or function in the Church. Thus, at the
present stage of thought on the subject, it is difficult to see
how some seminaries have been able in good conscience to
omit or gloss over mental prayer in favor of liturgical practices. But there is also an unhappy tendency to think of
these exercises as something immutable in form, frozen into
a particular mold, down to the last accidental quality. There
is much in the spiritual program of the seminary that can be
adapted and improved without altogether abandoning the
traditional and required exercises. Basically, such adaptations are something which each seminary will have to decide
for itself, with due regard to the situation of the diocese and
the age and development of the students.[1]

The most common flaw in most programs is the failure to
adapt the method of performing the spiritual exercises to

the age and condition of the students. Often, seminarians entering the college department for the first time are expected to make spiritual exercises identical in substance and form with those made by deacons. They are often discouraged by the failure to make progress or by their lack of understanding, and so they tend eventually to give up trying. This is particularly true of mental prayer. Would it be rash to estimate that this is the normal situation? or that the overwhelming majority of diocesan priests discontinue such practices as meditation and examen after ordination? If so, can this be blamed entirely on the priests themselves, or on their crowded schedules?

Let us use mental prayer as an example, and as typical of the others. Like all spiritual exercises, it is intended to perfect the individual as such, not merely as priest; it is a means to Christian, not just to clerical perfection. Its contribution to the good of the individual should begin as soon as the candidate enters the seminary. No one is going to claim that it is an easy undertaking, but on the other hand it is not beyond the capacity of the ordinary human being, otherwise the Church would never demand its daily use. Furthermore, it is derivative of the normal human functions of thought and introspection. Despite obstacles in individual cases, it is not a superhuman activity. There is no denying that periods of ineffectiveness (or aridities, as the spiritual authors call them) will arise, but it is up to the seminarian and his spiritual director to decide whether these periods constitute true aridities or whether they spring from some other source.

Mental prayer is intended to be prayer, not an exercise of blind obedience. Students are often told that half an hour of merely combating distractions is meritorious, and that perseverance through dry spells contributes greatly to their spiritual lives. True, but we must never forget that this prayer is not comparable to the meaningless acts of obedience of the anchorite—it is a human act which is intended to be a true encounter between a man and his God.

A partial source of this difficulty can be found in the failure to take account of normal human psychology. Any act of worship should be a sound psychological experience, because it arises from the very nature of man. When the human elements are allowed to languish or are neglected, the religious suffers accordingly. In its fullness, the liturgy is every bit as much an expression of human nature as it is of man's need to worship. Thus, when the liturgy became remote from human experience and understanding, the Church and its worship suffered in direct ratio.

For example, in very many seminaries, mental prayer takes place early in the morning, sometimes on the dubious principle that the most important exercises must be "gotten in" before breakfast or they are lost for the day. For this reason, meditation periods usually begin very early in the morning. While making all due allowances for the work of grace, it is still difficult to admit that the average human being is capable of arising in the early hours of the morning, and then of sitting in a chapel for half an hour or more while engaged in taxing mental concentration. To expect that a student who is not yet out of his teens will benefit from this is to presume a good deal. Likewise of dubious benefit are the complex and involved outlines sometimes offered to students as guides for their morning meditation.[2] If the meditation period is followed by Mass and thanksgiving, there may be a period up to an hour and a half long when the student is expected to be concentrating —and all before breakfast! This type of prayer life demands an almost miraculous endurance.

Much of this kind of scheduling is the result of the traditions of religious communities. In past ages, it was a normal thing for people to have much of their work done before dawn so as to take advantage of the daylight hours. Though such a schedule is still common in many religious communities, and derives from a simpler, agrarian society, it is time that it should be revised in the seminary, and this process of revision is taking place in many parts of the country.[3]

Another common criticism of the spiritual programs of seminaries is that they tend to equate spirituality with the performance of these exercises, or with mere attendance at them. Doubtless, the emphasis on making these exercises each day has at times led to the assumption that their performance equalled automatic holiness. Their omission was regarded as the beginning of a long concatenation of rejected graces and falls which inevitably would lead to the abandonment of the seminary or the priesthood. In such a milieu, formalism can become a pressing danger, and despite the insistence on "getting in" spiritualities, their omission was seldom accomplished by any real sense of loss.

This approach can also make these exercises very individualistic and self-centered. Such great emphasis is sometimes laid on what the person himself does that by omission his spirituality tends to develop independently of any concept of involvement with others or with the current life of the Church. It is possible for a person to think that his own personal holiness will draw down graces on others without his having to exert himself personally. Thomas' principle, *contemplata aliis tradere*, often stops at the first word in practice, if not in theory. In the small world of the seminary, the student can easily learn to forget that he develops as an individual who is an integral and important member of a body.[4]

The spiritual program of the seminary should aim, like all good teaching, at drawing the student from the simpler and easier to the more difficult. Since most students entering the years of college have had no previous experience with these things, they will need help. Instead of plunging them directly into silent meditation early in the morning, some type of group discussion can be used. Apostolic groups such as the Cursillo and the Action Catholique Ouvrière have found that group techniques which involve an articulation on the part of the individual regarding some aspect of the apostolate can be very successful. The ACO in particular, with its *revision de vie*, has found an apt instrument for helping its members gain a new focus on life, and for thinking through current problems in a Christian way.[5]

In the seminary, some adaptation of these techniques might be more effective even than having someone make an oral meditation for the students, for it would demand that the individual student formulate his own ideas and his own response. This approach could be used for perhaps two to four years, and would permit the student to be gradually weaned from group activity to a more private, individual prayer.

The psychological outlook of the modern adolescent would seem to demand less of this individual contemplation, at least at first, and more group communication. The value of this approach, long recognized in the behavioral sciences, is just beginning to have an influence on the Church. Certainly, seminaries could make good use of it. Some already have used group-dynamics sessions to great advantage to help students solve the more elementary and common problems of seminary life.

It should be remembered that a sound religious experience should also be a sound psychological experience. Far from attempting to set up psychological or human principles in place of spiritual ones, we should emphasize that religious exercises will be far more effective insofar as they are adapted and suited to the mentality and personality of the person making them. The Ignatian Exercises are probably the best known example of a psychologically sound spiritual method. The concept of a retreat, for example, as an extended period of total silence, complete recollection, introspection, and meditation, is not an absolute. "In silence and recollection the devout soul goes forward" is not an utterance of the divine law that allows no exceptions. In a properly group-centered situation, more may be accomplished in one hour than in many days of silence. A three-day retreat based on group communication, mutual help, and discussion, may do more for an individual than a week of sermons and private meditations.

To approach the entire question from a more positive point of view: what ideally should the spiritual formation program of any seminary seek to accomplish? In answer, it should be devoted primarily to the worship of God through the individual and collective actions of the seminarians and their faculty. It should try to sanctify the student both as an individual and as a social being. Insofar as he is an individual, it should try to secure from the seminarian the highest degree of response and commitment, and should provide ample opportunity for him to formulate this response and nurture this commitment. It should attempt to sanctify the entire day, rather than try to space the spiritual exercises for the purpose of leaving the rest of the day free for other activities. The daily schedule should be structured around the Mass, Lauds, and Vespers, as the determining elements. It should be adapted, as we have said, in the earlier years to the mentality and outlook of the modern adolescent. It should develop a spiritual life for the diocesan priest, rather than try to make him live as a religious in a parish.

In some ages, the liturgy admirably fulfilled these functions. It was an outstanding example of the meshing of the humanly appealing with the spiritual. Like Christ himself and like the Church itself, it was a blending of the human and the divine. And the liturgy, as the Second Vatican

Council has already decreed, should be the source from which the spiritual life of a seminary is derived.[6] It should be the binding force and integrating factor that unites and relates all the different acts of the spiritual program into one coherent and meaningful whole.

The phrase "integrating factor" needs close examination. It is not synonymous with quantity. Unfortunately, it is easy to confuse the integration of the spiritual program with the liturgy with a large number of liturgical practices. The liturgical spirit does not proceed automatically from a multitude of ritual acts. Not uncommonly, scriptural devotions, cushions in place of missal stands, altars facing the assembly, the use of contemporary art, whole-wheat hosts, and a measured use of jargon can deceive both faculty and students into thinking that externals are the real worship of the Church.

The seminary is a Christian microcosm. It is a small, rather complete, and largely isolated unit which, in its own way, reflects the Church at large. Within this microcosm, the students and faculty live both as individuals, each with his own problems and his own outlook, and as members of a community, a fact which adds dimension to their lives, brings them a new set of responsibilities, and provides the opportunity for even greater spiritual development by the fullest possible exercise of Christian charity and the formation of beneficial Christian relationships. In leading this communal life, the members have to relate and to adjust on a variety of levels. The liturgical-spiritual program of the seminary strives to show the student how to sanctify his

attitudes and relations toward others, and how to exercise
them from a supernatural point of view. This he must do
in union with all the other aspects of his training; the
spiritual life must, like all his other activities, be intrinsic
to his ordinary activities. Eventually, he will have to formulate similar relations with those outside the seminary.

Thus it is that the seminary seeks to provide an atmosphere in which the student will be free to exercise as much
as possible his baptismal and confirmational characters.
Like the Church at large, the individual student has been
set aside—chosen and elect—for the worship of God. As a
Christian, this is his highest duty; as a priest, this will be
the *raison d'être* of his vocation, the one in which, as an
instrument, he is elevated and actuated to produce an effect
beyond the power of any created nature. If the seminary
is truly to be a reflection of the Church universal, it must
be dedicated totally and completely to the worship of God.
If this is done, then the spirit of that worship will infallibly
permeate the other aspects of the seminary program, without the need of any artificial or external integration.

The sacrifice of the Mass is the core of this worship. It
occupies the paramount place, and everything else must
lead to it and derive from it. In this respect, though it is
asking some extra effort from administrators, the scheduling
of the Mass in the seminary order of the day must take
precedence over all else. It should determine the scheduling
of everything else, not vice versa. The actual time will vary
according to the good judgment of different administrators,
but it must always be at a time when, for students and

faculty alike, its place will be unmistakably first. It would seem that a scheduling late in the morning or early in the evening would be preferable; but regardless, the seminarian must find in it the culmination of everything that he has experienced up to that time and the direction for everything that he will do thereafter. Hence it is also better that nothing which would distract him from the meaning of the Mass should either precede or follow it. Participation, of course, should be both active and varied. This subject has been adequately treated by others, and for this reason we shall not go into detail on methods of participation or frequency.[7]

Mass should be followed by a period of reflection during which the student, at his leisure and for as long as he wishes, may meditate on the meaning of the act in which he has participated and draw conclusions and resolutions for application during the day. He must have some time to himself to place his day in its proper relation to the Eucharistic Sacrifice. This is not a thanksgiving period in the true sense of the term, for the Eucharist, by nature and by definition, is itself a thanksgiving. It is a time of personal response. The student should be encouraged to make this a period of brief, intensely personal meditation, rather than a time for reading some set prayers.

In this scheme of things, the place of Benediction may at first seem ambiguous, but it need not be. A true liturgical ceremony, Benediction is the expression of the supernatural instinct to worship Christ directly in the Eucharist, in contrast to the Mass whose essential orientation is worship of

God the Father through and with Christ. It should also be impressed on the seminarian that Benediction is a liturgical recalling of the Mass, a second blessing which resumes the first blessing, the Mass itself. Viewed in these lights, it does not become merely another spiritual exercise (and one whose liturgical purpose is often ignored), but rather a true liturgical recall to the Eucharistic Sacrifice and a complement to it. For this reason, if for no other, it should be held as frequently as possible.

The Breviary is the official daily prayerbook of the priest and a *fortiori* of the seminarian. The pivotal prayers of the Breviary, as the Council has pointed out, are Lauds and Vespers, the morning and evening prayer.[8] Vespers are usually sung in seminaries on Sundays and holy days, in accord with canon 1367, but it would be better if there were daily recitation of both Lauds and Vespers in English. Compline should be the final prayer of the day in immediate preparation for retiring—whether it should be recited in common or in private would be a matter for individual seminaries to decide, though private recitation would seem preferable because of the more personal nature of the Compline prayers. Other vocal prayers that the students recite during the day should be drawn as much as possible from the Breviary, the Scriptures, or some other liturgical source, for example the Collect of the day's Mass as the opening prayer for classes.

The reading of Scripture should be one indispensable practice. It would be wearisome to belabor once again how infrequently Scripture is either read or employed by the average priest. Yet every seminary order of the day should provide a period when the students read or have read to them passages from the Old and the New Testament. These sections should be coherent and integral, not random choices severed from their context. Nor would it be extraordinarily difficult to match the sections from each Testament so that parallel or complementary passages be read together. A sensible application of this would give the students a far deeper and more personal appreciation of the history of salvation than many classroom lectures. Such scriptural readings, or even many briefer ones, could be used to begin other spiritual exercises, or even classes and assemblies. Obviously, scriptural devotions should be held regularly, at least once every one or two weeks. It would perhaps be best if such devotions were held in relation to the Sunday Mass as a means of meditation and reflection on it. The same is to be said of frequent, even daily homilies at Mass.

In all these suggestions, two practical problems arise. First, what is the status of the other spiritual exercises of the seminary, such as spiritual reading, rosary, meditation, examen, and visits to the Blessed Sacrament? Their intrinsic value is obvious and, of course, they are required by canon 1367. But since they are "private" in nature, taking that term with all the cautions necessary, they should be made more private in practice. In the graduated discipline which is the ideal of every seminary, they could be held in common during the first two or three years of college for the purpose of implanting their habitual practice in the semi-

narians. But definitely for the years of theology, they should
be made privately, even in those circumstances in which
the seminary provides a time for their fulfillment.

The other problem is more difficult. The seminary is a
closed and artificial society, and in many ways it is monastic.
It definitely does not correspond to the life of a parish
priest. In the seminary, a man is a member of the community; in the parish, he is the leader. In the seminary, he
is a member of the liturgical assembly; in the parish, he is
the celebrant. But most of all in the seminary, his liturgical
practices are performed in common with others. In the
parish, this group environment may be lacking. The parish
may also lack many of the liturgical practices to which he
has grown accustomed, and it may fall far behind the
Church universal in developing a liturgical life. It should
be emphasized that the liturgical-spiritual program of the
seminary, as opposed to liturgical courses, is intended to
sanctify the student and mature him spiritually by offering
him the ideal means of worshipping God in common with
other members of the Mystical Body. It is *not* a course in
pastoral liturgy whose purpose is to accustom the student
to certain liturgical practices so that he can later introduce
them into his priestly work.

The liturgical program will carry out the Thomistic
principle previously cited: *contemplata aliis tradere*. The
liturgy must perfect a person, this particular individual, this
member of the Christian community. This person must
have an opportunity to make both a personal and a social
response to God. If this training has its proper effect, then

the priest will have a high regard for his own worth as an individual, he will find and appreciate this same worth in the people he serves, and he will appreciate his own position in the Church and the responsibilities it entails. His own personal development and degree of liturgical perfection and understanding will be of the greatest help in approaching his own parochial ministry and in building a spiritual life which is an integral part of it.

8

Of Freedom and Obedience

It has been predicted that the American Church will soon face a crisis of authority. Some feel that the "new breed" and the more traditionalist members of the hierarchy are destined to meet in open and perhaps permanently divisive conflict. Whether this is true or not only time will tell. But there can be no doubt that the problem of authority in the Church, or, to phrase it more precisely, the problem of the functioning and administration of authority, is one of the most perplexing and difficult of the present time.[1]

The problem is not new to the seminary. Anyone who has dealt with seminaries for any length of time knows that the crisis in authority is endemic and that it seems to worsen each year. The traditional approach to the problem of obedience and authority in the seminary has been both legalistic and militaristic. The seminarian has been reminded constantly that he is a functionary, part of a larger picture; that obedience to his bishop and pastor—and in the interim to the seminary authorities—is not only a *sine* qua non, but somehow the most important thing is his spiritual life. The bell has been the voice of God, and the rules the Holy Spirit speaking to him directly through human instrumentality. Obedience is the virtue that will supply for all the defects of the person commanding, and that will somehow make everything turn out all right in spite of human bungling.[2]

The seminarian is frequently and frankly told that he will be judged by the quality of his obedience and docility. "Let discipline, therefore, joyfully embraced, be the touchstone whereby superiors test the vocations of their students."[3] Not infrequently, this emphasis can obscure the need for other positive signs, and the situation that Joseph Fichter S.J. has described in religious communities can also be found in seminaries: "A trainee may be relatively incompetent, uninterested, or indifferent, concerning the various specific roles for which he is being prepared. This would not necessarily constitute doubt about his calling, or grounds for dismissal from the house of studies. Let him, however, indicate distaste or indifference for the community life of the seminary or novitiate and his vocation may be seriously called into question."[4] In the diocesan seminary, the obedient, quiet student who never causes any trouble may be easily ordained without ever giving any other sign of his potential effectiveness in the priesthood.

From the very beginning, we must emphasize that authority in the Church is not merely essential to its organization and nature (as would seem to be true in any society), but is God-given in the very literal sense of the word. The democratic process can encounter serious difficulties in the Church for the very simple reason that the constitution of the Church lends itself to an autocratic and absolute exercise of power.[5]

But God-given authority is not always exercised in a Christ-like manner. The problem of authority in the Church today, and a *fortiori* in the seminary, centers on the way in which it is carried out. Many have blamed this situation on the effects of the Constantinian era and the introduction of Roman Law into the life of the Church, or on the negative and legalistic aspects of the Catholic Reformation which intensified emphasis on the external nature and juridical organization of the Church. There is now a growing realization that the monarchical and hierarchical nature of the Church does not exclude consultation or the upward and downward communication between superior and subject. The history of the exercise of papal power, from Gregory VII to John XXIII, is proof of this. The basic equality and freedom of all Christians are not incompatible with hierarchical jurisdiction.

One of the more interesting aspects of this current reconsideration of authority is the similarity of conclusions reached by men working from different principles. There is a surprising parallel of judgments by Greeley and Fichter working from sociological studies, by Kennedy working from psychological principles, and by Rahner studying the question theologically. From the work of these men, certain trends can be discerned which can throw a great light on what seminary discipline should be.[6]

It is necessary to respect the integrity and conscience of the individual. The individual can no longer be considered a mere organizational cog whose only purpose is to obey or be directed. In our times, the Church has begun to re-ëmphasize the value of the person and his conscience, and there is a growing realization that coercion and so-called "blind" obedience, though they may produce a smoothly running and ostensibly efficient organization, do not necessarily create any personal commitment or change of heart.[7] "Professionals in the Church will do their best work in a situation where they have 'as much freedom and self-respect as possible,'" according to Greeley, and he adds a thought drawn from profound common sense: "God would not be pleased by anything that dehumanizes one of his rational creatures."[8]

If authority is to have greater respect for the individual, then conversely the individual must have greater respect for himself. It is not possible for a person to hide behind obedience as a means of escaping the responsibility for his own actions. Freedom is onerous, and one of its greatest burdens is the acceptance of responsibility for human acts and their foreseeable consequences.

A human being cannot relinquish his personality to a representative . . . the "just presumption" that the command of a superior is not only subjectively but also objectively morally unobjectionable does not constitute a simple dispensation from the essential obligation of every man to attain to moral certitude in regard to the free action he is about to perform. This action is no less his own and no less one for which he will be responsible, just because it is commanded. . . . The subject . . . has no right simply to take refuge behind obedience as if he could thus be free from a responsibility which he himself must bear, the responsible direction of his own personal initiative.[9]

Both superior and subject, then, must respect the subject's right and duty to be the responsible master of his actions.

There is no absolute equation between the will of the superior and the will of God. "The formal correctness of his [the superior's] commands does not guarantee that they are likewise ontologically guaranteed. If the subject must obey in order not to be disobedient before God, this fact is no proof that the command given was the command which, according to God's antecedent will, should have been given. It can be the product of a permitted fault in the superior."[10] This is probably one of the thorniest problems in the entire reëvaluation of the concept of authority and obedience; the equation of the superior's will and God's will is difficult to explain theologically. Many rebellious or frustrated seminarians, on being told that each rule represents the will of God, have perhaps been tempted to retort: "Prove it." But the fact should be faced that all too frequently the total equation of the will of the superior (and thus of the rules) with the will of God, even in the smallest matters, has merely been an excuse for those in authority not to justify their actions or to secure compliance with commands that are not well thought out. This kind of easy escape from the more difficult aspects of command, this convenient idea that obedience will make everything all right, has probably hurt the concept of obedience more than it has helped. It tends to produce passivity in the subject, and to shield him from the ultimate responsibility that he bears for his own actions.

It cannot be denied that the seminary authority, viewed globally and in general, is coincident with the divine will, but it is a serious mistake, at least psychologically, to look for a consequent divine rectification of every action, rational or rash, of the person exercising the authority. All too often, a seminarian who has been trained under such a system comes to realize the contradictions involved in carrying this concept too far, and is liable to reject the whole idea of authority and obedience, in practice if not in theory. It is the familiar case of the equal and opposite reaction.

This consideration leads logically to the next. *Those in authority should not be afraid to give reasons for what they command.* Rahner has expressed this idea succinctly: "The superior should not try to give the impression that he stands under the immediate inspiration of the Holy Ghost, but should be courageous enough to seek approval for his commands by giving reasons for them."[11] This does not vitiate obedience, but rather emphasizes its rational character. Many traditional spiritual reading books still used in seminaries exalt the obedience of the meaningless act, the watering-the-dry-stick-in-the-desert type of compliance which is supposed to be so pleasing to God as a perfect holocaust of the will. Even if such a concept can be defended in theory, it can well be asked how, in a society where compliance is no longer esteemed and even the direct command has grown rarer (witness the devious rituals used

by some corporations to discharge executives), such a concept can be relevant to the training of priests. It is characteristic of the modern seminarian that he seeks a rational
basis for his obedience, if not precisely as a reason for
obeying, at least so that he may obey in a more human
manner.

*There must be free communication between authority
and subject.* The Church has frequently absorbed ideas of
great value from without. Fichter and Greeley have shown
how much the Church can learn about the exercise of its
authority from modern corporate organizations and bureaucracies. "In the modern . . . organization blind obedience is
simply not enough."[12] In the contemporary organizational
structure, secular or religious, there must be a free flow of
information and ideas between those in command and
those in the lower echelons. Authority must be able to trust
itself to its subjects, to feel it can tell them the reasons why
things are commanded, why certain procedures are followed
rather than others. More important, subjects should feel
that they can confide in their superiors, that their ideas and
suggestions are not merely tolerated, but sought and valued.
A man must feel that he is an integral part of an organization, not a meaningless and lifeless part, not something dis-
pensable and easily replaceable. If a person does not feel
that he has such a place, his contribution and his obedience
will never measure up to his potential. His share of the
work will be lifeless.

Apropos of the executive, it has been said that he must
see "that information flows up the line of communications

so that he is able to make decisions, but he must also see that it flows down the line so that those who are to implement the decisions will be able to understand the reasons for it."[13] Consultation in any organization is most effective when "the people on the lower levels are persuaded that their honest opinions are wanted, will be listened to, and may have some effect on what is going to happen."[14] Rahner has phrased the same thought in different words: "Not to prevent his subjects from assuming initiative is not enough for a superior. He must positively count on it, invite it; he must not be irked by it."[15]

It is the duty of authority to motivate and encourage commitment and response. To inspire and obtain spontaneous and free compliance is perhaps the most difficult task that authority is called on to carry out, yet it is vital that it strive to secure the most intelligent kind of participation in the work of the group. It is also the task which in practice is most rarely attempted or attained. But it is precisely this type of obedience that the seminary should try to draw from the student, for this is the kind that will be of the greatest service at the parochial level; it is the kind which is most human and most Christian.[16]

It may be objected that in trying to apply these principles to the seminary, we are following certain trends of our present-day society too closely. Is, in fact, the current usage of authority in corporations a sound criterion for its usage in the seminary? In our opinion, it is, generally, for it is impossible to train seminarians in one fashion and expect them to behave toward their people in another. The days of the clerical tyrant and the absolutist pastor are clearly numbered if not entirely gone. The parish is neither a monastery nor a lay seminary. Within his parish, the priest must exercise the kind of authority that his people are used to, and which will draw the greatest response from them. If he does not, he will lose them. It is psychologically inconsistent to train a man with a rigid, monastic concept of authority, imbue him with instant and blind obedience, and then expect him to behave otherwise with his people. Furthermore, it seems more than likely that a newer approach based on these principles will be more successful with the present generation of students than the more traditional measures. No matter what the reason, it is certain that today's students do not easily accept rigid authority and unthinking obedience.

What has been said so far is very theoretical. There are other, practical aspects of this question which must be examined if we are to have an over-all view of the problem. The problem of authority, difficult enough in any environment, is compounded in the seminary. The physical isolation and the natural passivity engendered by discipline, rules, order of the day, and the emphasis laid on the preparatory nature of the seminarian's training, are but a small part of the difficulty. There is an apparent contradiction of purposes.

Anyone who looks objectively at the purposes of the seminary must honestly face the fact that it seems to be trying to do the impossible. On the one hand, every seminary wants to produce the priest who can think for himself, and to develop "the sense of responsibility, the capacity to use his judgment concerning men and events, and the spirit of initiative,"[17] who can think analytically and critically enough at least to discern truth from error, who can lead his people, accept new ideas, and utilize the good in current movements. Yet at the same time it is trying to form a man who can obey his bishop when final decisions are made, who can live with a domineering and unreasonable pastor, and who can demand adherence to principle when principle is at stake. Even the most superficial mind can see that the seminary is trying to teach apparent opposites at one and the same time. And we should stop to think before criticizing the seminary too severely for failing to achieve this ideal. Granted that the ideal is confused and that the seminary would like to exploit the best of apparently opposing qualities, such a failure becomes more understandable. The ideal has not been achieved, in the seminary or out of it, in the Church particular or universal, in religious or civil society. We fall short and always shall.

Let us pursue this consideration further. The seminary is obliged to train the seminarian for the actual life that he is going to lead in a specific diocese and, insofar as possible, in a particular type of parish. Not all the ideas of the aggiornamento have filtered down to the parish level. The assistant priest has to deal with a variety of pastors, many of whom may be completely unsympathetic to the more progressive ideas on authority. The future priest must be trained to live with such people, and similar types to be found among his parishioners, and to do so without patronizing

them. The seminarian must be able to accept authority
rationally and freely, to understand and exercise it in the
ways we have described; yet at the same time he must be
prepared to live under circumstances in which authority is
exercised arbitrarily, dogmatically, harshly, and without any
consideration of the individual.

Equally important, the candidate has to attain a certain
degree of maturity and has to form certain habits which
may go contrary to his nature, or in which he has little
natural interest. All the rational explanations in the world
may not suffice to make a lazy student diligent, a slovenly
student neat, or a tardy student punctual. Coercion must
be used at times, and it may be the providential means of
making an adequate vocation good, and a good vocation
better. Even the most independent-minded layman would
be grateful to the seminary for eradicating habits that he
finds repellent—even if it were done at the price of de-
priving the seminarian of some of his God-given freedom.
Any seminary dean who has ever tried to convince otherwise good students of the benefits of frequent showers or
cleaning his cassock or showing up on time for Mass will
understand this point very clearly. These are not considerations to be dismissed lightly, since it is minor points such
as these that draw the most barbed criticism from the
laity.

There is another very human point to be considered.
Many seminary administrators who are favorable to current
ideas on authority find it very difficult to carry them out in
practice. The reason is simply that many students take ad-

vantage of their new freedom, and seem incapable of being motivated to do what they ought. Those in authority tend to react by a sort of "backlash," and feel that all the theory is nebulous and impractical and that the old ways, for all their drawbacks, at least forced on the student a minimum observance. Thus, too, students who will demand that authority communicate reasons and decisions to them are often quite unwilling to do the same to those over them. This basic self-centeredness, nourished undoubtedly by the isolated environment of the seminary, alienates authority and brings discredit on the newer approaches. For the seminary administration, there must be a delicate balance of patience and severity which will be difficult to achieve, but which will in the end prove of great benefit.

What, then, if the student fails in his responsibility? It is our contention that the greater the freedom and leeway given the student, the more severely should his lapses be judged. If he fails to use his liberty properly, and if the seminary will not be a party to continued punitive measures, then the administration must be resolute and fearless in removing him. The common good of the seminary and the entire priestly state demand it. A more human and rational approach to discipline should not be construed as softness or relaxation of standards.

It is precisely the abuse of freedom that has many persons dubious about the bolder steps which have been taken in some seminaries. Most commonly cited is the tendency in many institutions to leave spiritual exercises, including attendance at daily Mass, to the discretion of the student.

One very disturbing innovation in several diocesan seminaries is that they permit their students on vacation freedom to date and attend dances up to the time of subdiaconate. A situation such as this makes it obvious that
after having discussed freedom, we should now say something about unfreedom.

Though there is great room for differences of opinion, it
must be recognized that there are areas where the student
can no more be free than the priest can. It is rather like a
hypothetical unfreedom, that is, within the context of a vocation and the supposition of a student's having freely embraced it, there are some things which he is obligated to do
and others which he is obligated not to do under pain of
violating his priestly commitment.

When a young man enters a seminary, he proposes to undertake a way of life in which certain acts of self-sacrifice
and certain acts of spirituality are an integral part. Whatever may be his freedom in individual instances, he does not
have the freedom, in the over-all picture, to back away from
that life if he wishes to remain in it. This is equally true of
those obligations which the student is preparing himself to
undertake. Thus, in the case of clerical celibacy, it is fatuous
for anyone to believe that any theological student can
have moral sexual freedom of this kind, and then at the
time of subdiaconate adopt a new way of life. The same is
true of Mass and the other spiritual exercises—though the
seminary may prefer not to coerce the student in individual
cases, it still has a grave obligation of knowing how he
carries out the externals of his spiritual life.

Obedience and discipline are not relatively new problems with seminarians, the result in part of the contemporary ferment of ideas in the Church and of modern permissive family life. These, of course, have helped to bring the problem of authority to crisis stage in some areas, but the truth is that seminarians have always disliked rules and restraints, and that obedience has always been a stumbling block. Perhaps the chief difference is that the contemporary seminarian is influenced by a factor unknown to his counterpart in the past—that is, in the present rethinking it is possible for him to find a theoretical justification for what he feels instinctively. The comments that we have made on authority are an example of what he can find to justify his complaints. He can find a rational basis in the increased discussion of the concept of freedom within the Church and of the necessity for avoiding legalism and petty restraints.

The seminarian who is in the first years of his professional preparation, that is, from the first year of college on, like his counterpart in the undergraduate school of any university, is searching for an identity. He is groping for maturity, for self-realization and security in his personality, and his experience in the seminary can hinder as well as aid this process. His isolation from a normal social environment can prevent complete maturation, while the emphasis on introspection can create self-doubts as well as self-knowledge. The gap between his concept of the priesthood and the form of life into which he enters can also generate a certain antagonism toward his external environment.[18]

Part of this maturation process is the working out of relationships to authority. The previous experience of most college-age students with this relationship has been the parent-child relation, however debased this may have become in some segments of our society. It is the authoritarian "father knows best" attitude with its heavy emphasis on direction and guidance. It presupposes maturity and development on the part of the parent, immaturity and growth on the part of the child.

When an adolescent enters the seminary, he is usually thrown into an authority-subject relationship which is closer to that which he experienced in his earlier years than it is to what he will experience in later life. While his counterpart in the liberal arts college is enjoying an increase of liberty, and molding relationships with a more distant, less personal authority, the seminarian is placed in a situation closer to that of a child toward his parents. The result is frequently regression, heightened by the newness and strangeness of his environment. He loses ground rather than makes progress. It is not unknown that students who, in their pubescent years, have had sexual difficulties such as masturbation and who have apparently conquered them, will suffer setbacks after entering the seminary.

Because of his mode of existence, the seminarian may take much longer in his total process of maturing than his counterpart in college. The first years of theology may often find him emotionally unprepared for his first steps toward the altar. One of the common complaints of seminary administrators is the childishness and immaturity of their students: their inability to make decisions, their gossiping and backbiting, their pettiness toward the faculty and toward each other, their boisterousness when outside the seminary, their romantic inability to see the more difficult side of life, and their assumption that they deserve the best of everything. The difficulty is to cure this outlook under the present system.

Thus it is that the newly ordained priest may find himself in the position of trying to work out problems and relationships that the ordinary person has solved in his college years. In new situations, he finds that the principles and guidelines given him in the seminary are not practical or were never thoroughly inculcated, and he then has to work out his own, frequently without any help. The most crucial period in the training of a priest is the first few years after ordination, the period that will "make or break" him as a priest. This is one of the sources of dissatisfaction with seminary training that Pius XII spoke of in *Menti Nostrae*.[19]

The seminary has to face the fact that many of the older approaches will not work now. The student wants and has a right to a rationale of his obedience. There must be a nexus between his intellect and his act of will. To try to bring about the latter without appealing to the former is self-defeating and contrary to human nature. Most of all, the student wants commanding integrity. He will accept the principle if he finds it embodied in a living person. He wants his reason appealed to, but he also wants a concrete image according to which he can form himself; and passive, docile, and automatic obedience makes a rather chilling image. No matter how much one may criticize his want as a departure from the ideal, the fact must be faced as a part of modern life.

Actually, the Church has always possessed the basic principle of freedom within an organization, a principle which has been reëmphasized in recent years in papal encyclicals.

It is a fundamental principle of social philosophy, fixed and unchangeable, that one should not withdraw from individuals and commit to the community what they can accomplish by their own enterprise and industry. So, too, it is an injustice and at the same time a grave evil and a disturbance of right order, to transfer to the large and higher collectivity functions which can be performed and provided for by lesser and subordinate bodies.[20]

This principle of subsidiarity is set forth principally for the social and economic order of nations, but there is no reason why it is not equally valid for that little world which is the seminary. Theoretically, the solution to the dilemma of obedience in the seminary is simple: the full implementation of this principle in every practical way. The seminary authorities should neither do for nor compel the students to do those things which they are quite capable of doing themselves. The delicate question is how to achieve this end. Administrators, not to say students, can and will have widely varying ideas of just how much the students are capable of doing on their own or how much they should be made to do.

The most direct way of applying the principle would be a complete reëvaluation of seminary life and discipline by each individual administration. If today's student demands a rational basis for his obedience, it is not a surrender on the part of the seminary authorities to try to find a rational basis for every aspect of its rules, discipline, and way of life. Certainly, anything in the seminary that is irrational, useless, or arbitrary, does more than merely irritate the seminarians; it defeats the whole purpose of the seminary.

All this means that everything in the seminary must have a real, but not necessarily immediate, relevance to the priesthood. It must lead to the priesthood, and it must help in some way to form the student for the particular work in the Church that he is going to be charged with. It must develop him as a human being and give leeway for the growth of those talents and abilities which will provide a suitable human basis on which his vocation can build and grow. This does not mean that the seminary is required to duplicate in every way the life of a priest. It simply means proportioning the means to the objective.

A good example of the application of this principle can be found in the order of the day. In how many seminaries, particularly in those operated by religious communities for dioceses, is the order of the day monastic in form? How many seminaries have ever arranged the seminarians' schedule in the light of the normal order followed by parish priests? How many seminaries have ever tried to read the trends of the times (for example, the hour of the celebration of Mass) and to establish a daily program accordingly?

The principle of subsidiarity will also dictate that the seminary must be ready and willing to revise its rules of discipline so as to eliminate what is petty and inconsequential, what is too detailed and stifling, and to harmonize them as much as possible with the spirit of the Gospels. Probably the predominant fault of seminary discipline has been the needless multiplication of small rules, and the rigid dictation of the time and manner of carrying out every function in the daily schedule. There should never be a rule without a proportionate reason, and where there is doubt it is better not to have the rule at all. This tendency toward a deadening and frustrating legalism is probably one of the worst legacies of the Catholic Reformation.

It is essential that the student be able to see this connection between his preparation and his goal. If his obedience is to be truly free and rational, he must know why he is doing something. He must see it as an integral part of his training for the priesthood, as a means of inculcating qualities he needs, of disciplining himself for a way of life that he has freely chosen. The well-intentioned student should be able to see the necessity of what he does, at least if it is explained to him. Great emphasis, therefore, must be laid on the student's personal commitment. He must be made to realize that he has chosen his vocation freely, and that he bears the basic responsibility for training and disciplining himself. He will be the kind of priest that he wants to be and little more. Every exercise of freedom that a seminary administration gives a student must be met by an equal degree of student responsibility. To use the popular expression, he must strengthen and develop his "I-Thou" relationship with God and, through it, the relationships that he will have with the people of God.

There must be genuine delegation of responsibility to the students themselves. This must go beyond the traditional mopping of floors or prefecting of the sacristy that many seminaries have considered a suitable preparation for exercising the responsibilities inherent in the priesthood. As far as possible, the students must be taught to govern themselves and, according to their age and capacities, be given the burden of directing or guiding others, as in some apostolic works.[21] Discipline and rules must be graduated. This self-evident principle, so well enunciated by Pius XII in *Menti Nostrae*, seems to have been largely unheeded in American seminaries.[22] It is doubtful that even half a dozen seminaries in this country have ever thoroughly examined their rules to see if they can gradually lighten restrictions as students grow older. In this regard, the lack of communication between different branches of even the same seminary can be appalling. Theologates may be stricter than college departments and more isolated. Even within the same department there is rarely any gradation of rules or regulations, even though a student in his senior year of college may be older and more mature than the student fresh from high school.

In this, more than in any other area of seminary training, there are no simple solutions. To carry out what has been suggested above, seminary administrators will have to be patient, tactful, determined, and more than a little understanding. The frustrations will be great, but will be more than justified by the improved atmosphere of the seminary.

9

The Seminary of Utopia

What would an ideal seminary be like? If we could be transported into a future of our own making, what kind of system would we establish for the training of priests?

One might imagine a large, metropolitan Catholic university—it does not have to be a Catholic university, but to keep the picture consistent we shall use a Catholic school. It is not much different from most Catholic universities in this country, except that it has a full and well-staffed department of theology, a large college church, and numerous dormitories which are houses of study for the dioceses of five or six different states.

In each of these houses dwell the seminarians who are studying at the university. They are under the immediate direction of priests from their own dioceses or, in the case of smaller dioceses or those with different traditions, they are directed by religious in interdiocesan dormitories. In all cases, the priests who are responsible for them, in addition to their priestly and academic training, have had two full years of preparation specifically for the task of guiding seminarians. This professional training has involved a thorough study of Church law regarding seminaries and seminarians, a year's study of adolescent psychology followed by a year of practical work with young people, and visits to different seminaries (including non-Catholic), to different professional schools, and even to military academies.

The diocesan house is presided over by the dean of students, who also functions as rector, and his assistants, including a sufficient number of full-time spiritual directors. Confessors are available from among these assistants, but some are also brought in each week for the convenience of the students. Generally, some of the clerical teachers from the university faculty also live in these houses, both to be available for consultation and to provide the seminarians with contact with a greater number of priests. The dean makes quarterly reports to the respective bishops on the status and conduct of each seminarian, after having made inquiries and sought advice from the student's teachers and from the other priests.

All the students, philosophers and theologians alike, attend classes at the university. There are no classes taught in the residence houses, and even those subjects which are strictly "seminary" subjects, such as pastoral liturgy or Canon Law, are open to all students, clerical and lay alike. Graduation from the undergraduate school of the university is a prerequisite for entrance into the school of theology. The major field of the undergraduate seminarian is determined by the student and his academic dean, with due con-

sideration being made for the young man's interests and the
needs of his diocese. Students with an accredited bachelor's
degree from another college may be received into the theological school also, but their advancement to minor orders
may be deferred. Failure to complete properly accredited
undergraduate work, that is, the lack of a bachelor's degree,
means automatic disbarment from theology. It is a prerequisite for the priesthood.

Summer school work is required after the completion of
the sophomore year of college. Students from rural dioceses
frequently use this time to study the specific problems of
their areas in such courses as rural sociology, or else they
spend part of their summer in actual field work. Students
from large metropolitan areas frequently do the same in the
fields of urban renewal, of the inner city, and of juvenile delinquency, but they may also take courses toward teaching
degrees, especially in dioceses which utilize their priests for
high school work. A similar program would be followed by
those students who may qualify for higher studies so as to
provide each diocese with a corps of experts in every field
from Scripture to sociology. However, for all students at
some stage of their professional training, the summer school
session will be devoted to workshops and institutes on
mental health, and to practical work with the mentally ill.

During the course of the school year, the seminarians may
also attend any of the lectures and institutes held on the
campus, whether sponsored by the university itself or individual houses of study. Similarly, the students are free to
make use of the various cultural and educational opportuni-

ties offered by the metropolitan area, such as libraries, special collections, museums, concerts, operas, etc. They are permitted full and total access to all news media that will keep them in contact with current events. Though the students do not join in all campus activities, they have frequent contact with the lay students, not only in class and at lectures, but also by joining them in study and discussion clubs.

This same interaction extends to many of the spiritual exercises. At seven o'clock in the morning, the seminarians of the various dioceses gather in the university church for the recitation of Lauds in English—and all lay students who wish to do so are free to join them. The community Mass is at noon and again all the students, clerical and lay, may participate. The daily homily concerns the Christian life in general and is applicable to both groups. The university schedule is such that all students are free to take part in the common English recitation of Vespers at 5:30 and in the Benediction that follows. After the Benediction, there is a brief period during which the seminarians examine their day and renew their resolutions. The seminarians recite Compline privately before retiring, and there is no lights out for any of the resident students. Spiritual reading and rosary are made in private. On Sundays, there is a scriptural service before the Solemn Mass which is at 11:00 A.M. After this comes the main meal of the day which, if possible, is common to all the students of the university as an additional sign of their unity after the Eucharist.

For the clerical students who are in the first two years of

their training, a colloquy is held three times a week with the spiritual director. Some question relating to Christian and priestly perfection is proposed and then discussed in common. It is concluded with a brief period of private prayer during which each one formulates his own particular response to the subject. On the other days of the week, the meditation is made privately, but at a common time. At the beginning of the third year of college, the meditation is entirely in private and at a time agreed on by the student and his spiritual director.

At the beginning of the first year of theology, the seminarian receives the first of his minor orders, the order of *theologian*. This elevates him to the clerical state and involves a twofold commitment: one to Christ, the Incarnate Word and the substantial revelation of the Father, the seminarian's model in all things; and one to the revealed word of God which is to be the object of his studies throughout the next four years. Thus he hands himself over to Christ who as the revelation of God the Father to man is the summit of human history, and to the study of his message, because he is seeking to be the dispenser of the mysteries of God. He strives to be a theologian in the complete sense of the term.

At the conclusion of second theology, he is promoted to the order of *reader*. This brings with it the power of preaching under supervision, so that he is now able to communicate in a limited manner the word which he has been studying. This also permits him to lead simpler services such as Scripture vigils and novenas.

At the beginning of third theology, the aspirant is pro-

moted to the order of *subdiaconate* together with its obligations of celibacy and the Breviary. *Diaconate* is conferred at
the conclusion of third theology and gives all powers which
do not require the power of order and jurisdiction of the
priesthood. This means that during his last year of study,
the seminarian is the ordinary minister of solemn baptism
and the administration of communion, he can give all the
unreserved blessings of the Roman Ritual, and he is empowered to be celebrant at Benediction, and to be the ordinary preacher to the Christian people.

In all this, of course, it would be our hope that all the suggestions and criticisms that have been made throughout this
book would be incorporated and implemented. None of it
would be a definitive and final solution. New problems will
inevitably arise, and new approaches will have to be sought
and found. The process of renewal in the seminary, like that
in the Church at large, must never cease.

What is it, in brief, that we have been trying to suggest?
Generally, we have proposed an end to the isolation which
has been characteristic of seminaries for many centuries and
a greater incorporation into the mainstream of modern
American life. This would entail a greater decentralization
of seminary administration, with more authority being
vested in the regional association of bishops, and the formulation of a general charter of administration for all seminaries. This decentralization would extend to each seminary, where less power would be given to the rector and a
greater voice would be given to the faculty as a whole.
Seminary administration in general should be more stand-

ardized; this should be carried out by the regional association of bishops and should be preceded by a thorough and comprehensive study of the present effectiveness of our seminaries. Reorganization would also entail the final abandonment of the 6-6 system of training and accreditation by regional and state agencies.

Within the seminary itself there should be a greater tolerance for and emphasis on the dignity and responsibility of the individual seminarian, with a consequent deëmphasis of petty restrictions and rules. The daily order of seminaries should have a greater orientation toward parish life. The extra liberty given to seminarians should be coupled with an intense effort to secure their total commitment to their vocation, particularly through the development of a liturgically oriented spiritual formation program which would aim at instilling a truly priestly and diocesan spirituality, not merely an adaptation of the religious life. There should be higher academic standards and the adoption of more uniform admission and dismissal policies. The American Church should also attempt to emphasize the special nature of the vocation to teach in seminaries, and develop a program of preparation geared especially to this work.

Above all, the Church in this country should put an end to the multiplication of small and inefficient seminaries. It should seek to coalesce those now in existence and, as far as possible, reunite the training of the priest with the training of the Catholic layman.

Appendix

Some Thoughts on the Problem of Perseverance

The role of the seminary in the perseverance of vocations has never really been adequately studied. The very few articles that have been written on the subject either deal with the student rather than with the entire picture, or they skim over the real causes of nonperseverance altogether. Everything from patriotism to the devil has been blamed for the alarming number of dropouts in the seminary, but only in the rarest cases has the system itself been blamed.[1] The general assumption has been that the aspirant must take the seminary as he finds it, and if he fails to survive the fault is entirely his own.

What has already been said in these pages about the nature of today's student and about the seminary can give some clues about the problem of nonperseverance, even if it will not provide any immediate solutions.

More than one seminary administrator has been appalled by the worst aspect of this question. The students who fail to persevere are often among the best, both intellectually and spiritually. Of course, for years many seminary men have been preaching that it is the good average student who makes the best priest. Does he really, and, if so, why? Other things being equal, the more talented and intelligent student should make the better priest, for grace, we are told, builds on nature. Frequently, the dropout of the brilliant and talented is looked on as the grace of God weeding out the troublesome, proud, and intractable. But it may also be weeding out the cultured, the inventive, the original, and the leaders.[2]

This attitude can become as classic an excuse for cultivating mediocrity as "the poor you have always with you" once became for social injustice. Seminaries have often been guilty of glorifying the average, and from there it is only a short step to condoning the mediocre. This plus the isolated atmosphere, the not infrequently uninspired and ill-prepared teachers, the petty rules and the constant surveillance, can produce acedia, that dangerous ennui compounded of frustration, boredom, apathy, and suffocated ideals. This sense of pointlessness is based on the lack of challenge offered by teachers and curriculum, on the inability of the student to feel that he is making any progress, on the failure of the seminary to give him the feeling that he is growing and developing as a mature human being. The seminarian spends too many years in a small-minded, minutely circumscribed, and intellectually sterile environment. The purpose of the seminary is to develop, not hinder, a vocation. This imposes on it the obligation of developing the seminarian precisely as human being: intellectual, volitional, esthetic, and physical. A seminarian is a man, and man needs a sense of accomplishment. To expect a student to work for years without real challenge and without the feeling of progressing toward an ideal is to demand a miracle in the moral order.

There are partial solutions to the problem. Entrance standards which bear a realistic relation to the academic demands of the seminary will prevent the entrance of students who will surely fail to meet these demands. This will help keep the over-all number of dropouts down and thus reduce the number of departures. Orientation programs for students entering for the first time can smooth over the difficult transition from family to institutional life. Seminars and group counseling can solve some of the commoner problems before they become too aggravated, and will give members of the seminary staff an opportunity to foresee troublesome situations. Lecturers and other contacts from outside the seminary can also help the student to identify with his vocation.

Many seminary authorities feel that an effective solution to the problem of acedia is a program of apostolic works. Many such programs have been initiated, and in many cases quite successfully, in many seminaries throughout the country, and if the present trend continues, it will become fairly universal. These usually include such activities as teaching religion, tutoring under-achieving students in depressed areas, visiting hospitals, working with the mentally ill, youth work of all sorts, helping with parochial liturgical programs, vocation work among grammar and high school students, and even the writing and producing of religious radio programs. This is a practical aspect of seminary training that is essential to a well-rounded program. And if such a program is well-planned, complete with preliminary instruction and follow-up seminars, it would undoubtedly do a great deal to save vocations.

There is one thing that definitely needs to be reformed. In the early Church, internship and training were provided by the minor orders and subdiaconate (see Chapter 2). Their purpose was—and theoretically still is—to introduce the candidate gradually into the exercise of ecclesiastical offices.[3] However, over the centuries these orders which were once so very practical and immediate have become entirely symbolic. At the time of tonsure, the cleric is told that he now wears the surplice by right because he is a member of the clerical state, even though he may have been wearing the cassock as a seminarian for years (and before that as an altar boy). As an acolyte, he is empowered to serve at the altar, though he may have been doing so since the fifth grade.

In the previous chapter, we indicated what the Church could well do in this revolutionary age: restore the minor orders to their pristine importance. This would necessitate the abolition of the system as we now know it, and the substitution of others, along the lines pictured in our discussion of the utopian seminary. To these orders would be attached genuine powers and functions, true duties to be exercised for the benefit of the people of God, and through which the seminarian could prepare himself for the priesthood.

Not infrequently, the seminarians themselves feel a great deal of confusion about what the primary function of a priest in modern society is. They may study counseling techniques or social sciences and feel that many of these functions—guidance, counseling, social work, delinquency control—are a fertile field for priestly work. Yet at the same time they are learning that in the modern world much of this work has been appropriated by lay, secular, and governmental agencies. The priest was once the only counselor and advisor to whom the ordinary Catholic could turn, now there are others. The Church was once the natural focus of the poor seeking help, but now they can easily turn elsewhere. The priest is no longer the only well-educated man in the parish, nor is he the sole educator—some parochial schools are staffed almost entirely by laymen.

Even in the area of liturgy and preaching, in those areas which demand the use of the specifically priestly character imparted by Holy Orders, there is a decreasing emphasis on the celebrant and the preacher, and a greater orientation toward the worshipping assembly. It is not at all surprising, then, that the idealism of the modern young man can so easily find an outlet—and sometimes a much better use—in areas and services which are neither priestly nor Catholic. And many of today's young men definitely feel that they can make a greater contribution to Catholic social action and to the spread of Catholic principles by undertaking a vocation outside the priesthood, for example service in the Peace Corps or as Papal Volunteers, or by being a Catholic faculty member at a state university.

This tendency is heightened by a factor extrinsic to the seminary itself, yet one which has distressing effects within

it: the image of the priesthood that the seminarian may receive in his own parish. He may find the life of the average
assistant pastor unappealing, particularly if the seminarian
himself is of above average intelligence or talent. The
thought of living with a lazy or unprogressive pastor, the
dreary administrative work, much of which does not require
a priest for its accomplishment, the loneliness, the often
narrow and petty authoritarianism, may easily chill his ideals
of the priestly life. In larger dioceses, he must often face a
deadening seniority system—a practice contrary to both the
mind of the Church and common sense—which keeps the
talented man out of authority until he has passed his most
creative years.[4]

Finally, the perseverance of seminarians can be achieved
only with the cooperation and help of a dedicated faculty.
The seminary faculty member is above all the one priest
with whom the seminarian has closest contact outside the
parish, and from whom he derives his ideas of the priesthood. Unlike the parish priest, the seminary priest is the
man available for comparison and estimation as the seminarian learns the theory of what a priest should be. If the
faculty member is frustrated, if his ideals are crushed by
one-man government and autocracy from above, if he lacks
academic freedom, if he is confined within a small and petty
world, his problems and attitudes will necessarily affect the
student's outlook. What is lacking in the seminary faculty
will inevitably be lacking in the seminarians.

Footnotes

¹ John Tracy Ellis, "Anti-Clericalism in America Today," *Catholic Messenger*, volume 80, (June 7, 1962). Replies can be found in the same volume (July 5, 1962). The best summary of his ideas can be found in the London *Tablet*, June 2, 1962, 532.

Daniel Callahan, "Lay-Clergy Tensions," *Ave Maria*, volume 96, (December 29, 1962), 8–9.

———, "Problems and Possibilities," *Commonweal*, volume 76, (August 10, 1962), 439–441.

Thurston N. Davis S.J., "Anti-Clerical Virus," *America*, volume 107, (June 16, 1962), 402–404. Ellis' comments on this article can be found in the same volume (July 7, 1962), 451.

I am inclined to agree with Callahan that native American anti-clericalism will not be of the virulent species it has been in Latin countries. The causes are different. It will be the product of "thwarted aspirations" which will result in the laity's turning away from the clergy and the works of the Church. It would relegate the clergy to a purely sacramental role which would have little effect on the life of the average Catholic.

² For example, Kenneth Eberhard's "What Seminaries Don't Teach," *Ave Maria*, volume 98, (July 13, 1963), 13–14.

³ *Time*, volume 84, (August 21, 1964), 40. Rather understandably, the editors of *Time* were unable to give the source of their estimate on the number of former priests in the United States. However, in a letter to the author, they did indicate that it was a

former priest who is now in good lay standing, who holds no bitterness because of his position, but who left the priesthood because of disputes with ultra-conservative superiors. Because of information received from confidential sources which I consider reliable, I believe that *Time's* estimate is generally accurate. However, in fairness it must be noted that such an estimate would span a large number of years. A dispassionate and objective treatment of this question can be found in Joseph Fichter S.J., *Religion as an Occupation*, Notre Dame 1961, 204–210.

⁴ This can be found in McAllister and Vandervelt, "Factors in Mental Illness among Hospitalized Clergy," *Journal of Nervous and Mental Diseases*, volume 132, (1961), 80–81.

⁵ An excellent treatment of the seminary environment is Eugene Kennedy M.M., "Differentiated Discipline in the Seminary," *Bulletin of the National Catholic Educational Association* (August, 1964), 79–85.

⁶ "There is at least some reason to think that the Catholic layman views his pastor primarily as an administrator of a large plant and the superintendent of an educational institution. The curate is looked upon as a part-time recreational supervisor and a part-time, bargain-basement psychiatric counselor." Andrew Greeley, *The Church and the Suburbs*, New York 1957, 72.

⁷ Daniel Callahan, *The Mind of the Catholic Layman*, New York 1963, 142.

⁸ Giles Lytton Strachey, *Eminent Victorians*, New York n.d., "Cardinal Manning," 65.

Callahan, *Mind of the Catholic Layman*, 131ff. This section was printed as "The Freedom of Priests," *Commonweal*, volume 79, (October 18, 1963), 95–98.

Spalding is quoted by Richard Hofstadter in *Anti-Intellectualism in American Life*, New York 1963, 138. Spalding was no anti-intellectual, but was merely citing conditions as they existed.

⁹ Sacred Congregation of Seminaries and Universities: Circular Letter on the First Centenary of the Death of the Curé of Ars, June 5, 1959, and Circular Letter on the Third Centenary of the Death of St. Vincent de Paul, September 27, 1960.

¹⁰ For a brief summary of the idea that seminary reform may "make or break" the Second Vatican Council, see "Seminary Reform," *America*, volume 109, (November 16, 1963), 626.

CHAPTER 2

¹ There are no formal histories of the seminary as such that are readily available, and even the standard Church histories tend either to neglect the subject or to scatter it piecemeal throughout many volumes. An excellent summary of the pre-Tridentine legislation can be found in James A. O'Donohoe, *Tridentine Seminary Legislation: Its Sources and its Formation*, Louvain 1957, 1–16. An adequate but dated summary can be found in the *Catholic Encylopedia*. For a good coverage of the background from which seminaries emerged, the following are helpful:

Pierre Coste C.M., *Saint Vincent de Paul*, Westminster 1952, volume 2, chapter 30.

Edward Healy Thompson, *The Life of Jean-Jacques Olier*, London 1886.

R. M, Rayner, *European History: 1648–1789*, London 1952.

Carl J. Friedrich, *The Age of the Baroque: 1610–1660*, New York 1952.

Henri Daniel-Rops, *The Church in the Seventeenth Century*, New York 1963.

An excellent summary of Counter-reformation religious attitudes can be found in Justus George Lawler, *The Catholic Dimension in Higher Education*, Westminster 1959, chapter 2.

² O'Donohoe, 2.

³ *Ibid.*, 3.

⁴ Gregory of Tours (?538–594), author of *History of the Franks*, is generally considered as representative of the decline of letters in the chaos that followed the break-up of the Western Empire. His Latinity is crude and ungrammatical, his thought is simple, superstitious, and credulous, and he is generally a far cry from the tradition of the great Western Fathers. See Henri Daniel-Rops, *The Church in the Dark Ages*, New York 1959, 250–251.

⁵ For a very fine study of the part played by the Church in the

restoration of Europe and the difficulties that it encountered, see Christopher Dawson, *The Making of Europe*, New York 1952.

[6] For the part played by the cathedral schools, see O'Donohoe, 11.

[7] *Ibid.*, 12.

[8] This quotation, as well as the one from Courtin, can be found in Coste, *Saint Vincent de Paul*, volume 1, 246–247. Vincent went on to say: "There was no special place in which these things were taught; a man, after his theology, his philosophy, his minor studies and a little Latin, went to a parish and administered the sacraments just as he fancied."

[9] The complete decree in English can be found in H. J. Schroeder S.J., *Canons and Decrees of the Council of Trent*, St. Louis 1941, 175ff.

[10] This latitude seems to have been intentional. See O'Donohoe, 150.

[11] Among the dioceses whose clergy was directly affected at some time in the nineteenth and twentieth centuries by the disciples of Olier and Vincent were St. Louis, New Orleans, San Francisco, Los Angeles, Brooklyn, New York, Boston, Buffalo, Philadelphia, Chicago, Houston, San Antonio, Denver, and Oklahoma City.

[12] Thomas Münzer, an ex-Franciscan turned Anabaptist, rose to prominence in the messianic and apocalyptic atmosphere that coincided with the first period of Luther's work. He tried to establish a theocratic kingdom of God at the Saxon village of Zwickau where wealth and property were shared in common and a revivalistic and emotional atmosphere prevailed. He was killed in the suppression of the Peasants' Revolt in 1524. See Roland H. Bainton, *Here I Stand*, New York 1957, 214–221.

John of Leyden, like Münzer, was an Anabaptist intent on setting up a worldly kingdom of God. In 1534–1535, he established a theocratic rule at Münster which quickly degenerated into a communistic dictatorship. The bizarre and manic activities of John and his followers—among whom the promulgation of compulsory polygamy in which John "the prophet" set the example by taking sixteen wives—led to the siege and capture of Münster by the local nobles. John of Leyden was captured, tortured, and killed.

[13] Cardinal Gian Pietro Caraffa represented the puritanical and

reactionary side of the Catholic Reformation. A reformer from his early years, he helped to found the Order of Theatines with Cajetan of Thiene, but he did not share the mild and meek disposition of that saint. A volcanic and impetuous man, he would brook no opposition to the progress of reform as he saw it. As Pope Paul IV, from 1555 to 1559, he gave full sway to the Inquisition, forcibly cleared the Papal States of brigands, and thoroughly cleansed Rome and the papal court by ordering absentee bishops to leave the city, and by sentencing idle and contumacious monks to the galleys. The Council of Trent did not meet during his pontificate, since he had little use or need for deliberative bodies. His reign was marked by a high degree of witch hunting in which such persons as Cardinal Pole, Archbishop Carranza of Toledo, and even his own Theatines fell under the disfavor of the Inquisition. See Philip Hughes, A Popular History of the Reformation, New York 1956, 283–284.

[14] For Ignatius' concept of obedience and some of the early difficulties that it caused, see Paul Dudon-William Young, Saint Ignatius of Loyola, Milwaukee 1949, 225, 229, 341, 343.

[15] Thus Sforza Pallavicino S.J., Istoria del Concilio di Trento, Milan 1844, volume 5, 469.

[16] See George Hagmaier's references in "Today's Religious Candidate: Psychological and Emotional Considerations," Bulletin of the National Catholic Educational Association (August, 1962), 111.

[17] A good example of this concept of authority is the famous maxims of Jacques Benigne Bossuet, Bishop of Meaux and famous preacher in the France of Louis XIV:

1) The king is sacred because he is anointed at the time of coronation by the priests of the Church, and hence it is blasphemy and sacrilege to assail the person of the king or to conspire against him.

2) He is in a very real sense the father of his people, the paternal king, and therefore it belongs to him to provide for the welfare of the nation.

3) His power is absolute and autocratic, and for its exercise he is accountable to God alone; no man on earth may rightfully resist the royal commands, and the only recourse for subjects against an evil king is to pray God that his heart be changed.

4) Greater reason is given to a king than to anyone else; the king is an earthly image of God's majesty and it is wrong, therefore, to look upon him as a mere man.

Summarized by Carlton J. H. Hayes, *A Political and Cultural History of Modern Europe*, New York 1944, volume 1, 291.

[18] For a good study of the exuberance of the Baroque in art, see Wylie Sypher, *Four Stages of Renaissance Style*, New York 1955.

[19] For the Baroque attitude toward liturgy, see Louis Bouyer, *Liturgical Piety*, Notre Dame 1954, chapter 1.

[20] For a modern comment on Vincent's originality and his "holy cunning," see Cardinal Leo Suenens, *The Nun in the Modern World*, Westminster 1963, 39.

[21] Thompson, *Olier*, 447.

[22] *Ibid.*, 463. That Vincent was torn between his conviction of the need of learned priests and his suspicion of intellectualism is evident from the following comment by Coste, volume 2, 183.

Although Saint Vincent's type of mind was practical, he had the highest esteem of knowledge and learned men. His diplomas of Bachelor of Theology and Licentiate of Canon Law, his close relations with the doctors of the Sorbonne . . . and still more his writings against the errors of his time, clearly prove this fact, against which Jansenist calumnies will ever prove unavailing. But what is true, and this cannot be levelled as a reproach, is that virtue was in his eyes superior to knowledge; virtue played a greater part in the conversion of heretics than theological learning, and knowledge without virtue was practically sterile and even dangerous. "Knowledge is essential," he said to his disciples, "and woe to those who do not employ their time profitably! But let us fear, let us fear, and I even venture to say, let us tremble a thousand times more than I can express; for those who are intellectual have much to fear: *scientia inflat.*"

[23] However, Daniel-Rops does call his first seminary rules "draconian." See *The Church in the Seventeenth Century*, 28. For a summary of these rules, see Coste, volume 2, chapter 30.

[24] Thompson, *Olier*, 450.

[25] This material is taken from the article, "A New Dimension in the Church," by James Hennesey S.J., *America*, volume 111, (October 7, 1964), 448–455.

[26] This was also true of many American colleges and universities, an illustration perhaps of the enduring American conviction of the superiority of rural values to urban.

[27] "[The Catholic Church] has failed to develop an intellectual tradition in America or to produce its own class of intellectuals capable either of exercising authority among Catholics or of mediating between the Catholic mind and the secular or Protestant mind. Instead, American Catholicism has devoted itself alternately to denouncing the aspects of American life it could not approve and imitating more acceptable aspects in order to surmount its minority complex and 'americanize' itself." Hofstadter, 136.

[28] On the lack of give and take in the classroom and the generally unexciting intellectual atmosphere of seminaries, see Gerard S. Sloyan, "Seminaries in America," *Commonweal*, volume 73, (October 7, 1960), 37–40.

[29] Preaching at the anniversary of the Mount Angel Seminaries in Seattle, John Tracy Ellis quoted Archbishop John Carroll's advice to an American priest studying in Paris: "This immense advantage [imbibing the spirit of Saint-Sulpice] will be for you and for the Church in the United States infinitely preferable to all the knowledge that you can acquire during your sojourn in Europe." *Catholic Sentinel*, (May 15, 1964), 15.

[30] For a consideration of the legal aspects of the 6-6 and the 4-4-4 systems, see Basil Frison C.M.F., "The 6-6 Program for Seminary Training," *The Jurist*, volume 19, (October, 1959), 502–511.

[31] Eugene I. Van Antwerp S.S., "Progress and Prospects in Seminary Administration," *Bulletin of the National Catholic Educational Association*, (August, 1963), 73.

CHAPTER 3

[1] All the various laws and determinations of the Church concerning the training of clerics have been collected in the *Enchiridion Clericorum: Documenta Ecclesiae Sacrorum Alumnis Instituendis*,

published by the Sacred Congregation of Seminaries and Universities (Typis Polyglottis Vaticanis 1938). It is dated, and suffers from using a chronological approach, which makes it difficult to study individual aspects of seminary government.

For a summary of all the elements that enter into seminary administration, see Edward F. Riley C.M., "An Analysis and Evaluation of Seminary Administration," *Bulletin of the National Catholic Educational Association*, (August, 1962), 69–75.

² Canon 1354, #1, 2, 3. Apostolic Letter of Pius XI, August 1, 1922, in T. Lincoln Bouscaren S.J., *Canon Law Digest*, Milwaukee 1934, volume 1, 646–647.

³ Canon 1357, #1, 2, 3.

⁴ Canon 1367.

⁵ Canon 1359, #1–4.

⁶ Canon 1358. Circular Letter of the Sacred Congregation of Seminaries and Universities to the Bishops of Portugal, September 8, 1935, *Enchiridion*, #1354, 1355.

⁷ Canon 1369, #1–3, and canon 1360, #1.

⁸ Circular Letter of the Sacred Congregation of Seminaries and Universities to the Bishops of Germany, October 9, 1922, *Enchiridion*, #1120. Regarding confessions, see canon 891. "The master of novices and his assistant, the superior of a seminary or college, are not to hear the sacramental confessions of their students who live with them in the same house unless the students, freely and from a grave and urgent cause in particular cases should request it."

On the responsibility of the rector, see the Instruction of the Sacred Congregation of Sacraments, December 27, 1930, *Enchiridion*, #1288, and the scrutiny required before the conferral of Orders, *Digest*, volume 1, 467–482.

⁹ Circular Letter of the Sacred Congregation of Seminaries and Universities to the Bishops of the United States, January 24, 1928, *Digest*, volume 1, 650. An excellent summary of the canonical requirements and qualifications of the spiritual director in a diocesan seminary can be found in Anthony J. Falanga C.M., "Spiritual Director," *Vincentian Educational Newsletter*, volume IV, (March, 1964), 1ff. Most of the matter here has been taken from that article.

The spiritual director's independence of external discipline has been repeatedly stressed. The letter to the Bishops of the United States emphasize this, as does a similar letter to the Bishops of Germany, cited in note 8. The triennial report of seminaries to the Sacred Congregation of Seminaries and Universities requires that he be *"nullo alio officio implicatus,"* Acta Apostolicae Sedis, volume 17, 549.

¹⁰ Circular Letter to the Bishops of the United States, Digest, volume 1, 650–651.

¹¹ Canon 1361, #1. Pius XI, Letter on Seminaries and Clerical Studies, August 1, 1922, Digest, volume 1, 644. Canon 1363, #1–3. Joint decree of the Sacred Congregation of Seminaries and Universities and the Sacred Congregation of Religious, July 25, 1940, Digest, volume 2, 426. A similar decree was issued by the Sacred Congregation of Seminaries and Universities alone on July 12, 1957; see Nicholas Gill C.P., "The Transfer of Seminarians," The Jurist, volume 20, (July, 1960), 338–340. See also the subsequent clarification by the Congregation in Digest, volume 5, 635.

¹² Canon 1363.

¹³ Canon 1371. Ad Catholici Sacerdotii, St. Meinrad 1944, 66.

¹⁴ Private Circular Letter of the Sacred Congregation of the Sacraments, December 27, 1957, Digest, volume 4, 303.

¹⁵ Ad Catholici Sacerdotii.

¹⁶ Instruction of the Sacred Congregation of Sacraments, December 27, 1930, Digest, volume 1, 463. See also Joseph J. Comyns C.SS.R., J.C.D., Canonical Determination of the Fitness of Candidates for Sacred Orders, Washington 1958.

CHAPTER 4

¹ For a general description of the elements that make up a vocation, with special emphasis on the need for commitment, see R. Klaver's "Why Do Seminarians Leave the Seminary?" Homiletic and Pastoral Review, volume 62, (October, 1961), 36–46. Unfortunately, the article does not answer the question in the title. One of the better treatments of the modern Catholic college student is Andrew Greeley, Strangers in the House, New York 1961, which

he has revised somewhat in "The New Breed," *America*, volume 110, (May 23, 1964), 706–708. An excellent accompanying article in the same issue is Donald R. Campion's "New World, New Church," 709–711.

An outstanding technical study is the report by the Jesuit Educational Association Workshop, 1962, edited by Robert J. Henle S.J., and privately printed by the Jesuit Educational Association. It has recently been published as *Christian Wisdom and Christian Formation* under the editorship of J. Barry McGannon S.J., Bernard J. Cooke S.J., and George P. Klubertanz S.J., New York 1964.

² This is a crucial point, easily overlooked by seminary administrators. It is important to remember that the "youth who comes for ecclesiastical studies, though he is seventeen years old chronologically, may be at almost any stage of emotional development." See Eamonn F. O'Doherty, "Emotional Development of the Ecclesiastical Student," *Doctrine and Life*, volume 12, (August, 1962), 411–421, condensed in *Theology Digest*, volume II, (Fall, 1963), 181–185. The purpose of adolescence, according to O'Doherty, is to determine identity, role, and status. "Achieving identity means discovering one's autonomy as a person, learning both the strengths and weaknesses of one's personality and the meaning of human consciousness with its consequences in self-initiated action." The maturing process in the college years generally centers around the male-female relationship and preparation for marriage, the subject-authority relationship, and the entire adjustment necessary in assuming a self-supporting and breadwinning role.

The aforementioned Jesuit survey phrases it in the following way. "His [the undergraduate's] problems, attitudes, and dispositions group around three major aspects of his maturing: 1) the discovery in some instances, the discernment in all, of his own personal lineaments with all their capabilities and powers; 2) the design of his ideals or, it may be, the rediscovery and reiteration of former ones under a new guise; 3) the development of individual autonomy or self-possession." See 318–319.

³ "It is imperative in our dealings with the present . . . college undergraduate to point out the reasons behind the procedure, the

regimen and the training; to explain fully the rationale of authority and the reasonableness of civil and ecclesiastical obedience." *Ibid.*

CHAPTER 5

[1] *Ad Catholici Sacerdotii* 63–64. Some very interesting norms for seminary teachers in religious communities can be found in the apostolic constitution *Sedes Sapientiae*, and can be applied, *mutatis mutandis*, to the diocesan seminary faculty. It reiterates that these men should be the best in the community, that they be distinguished for their zeal and knowledge, that "they are to know thoroughly the subject they teach, be well versed in it, and fully conversant with its research methods." They are to have the proper academic degrees, they must have "pedagogical and teaching talent," and they should have sufficient leisure "so that they can further their own learning and produce from it useful writings." See *The Apostolic Constitution Sedes Sapientiae and the General Statutes*, Washington 1957, article 30, paragraphs 1–4 incl.

A letter of the Sacred Congregation of Seminaries and Universities, January 25, 1928, states that seminary faculty members in the fulfillment of their duties "should not be unduly preoccupied by distractions of an economic nature and should be able to obtain the means necessary to develop and perfect themselves in their chosen fields of study." For this reason, bishops are to consider the opportuness of establishing suitable and progressively increasing salary scales, "so that the salary given will assure to each professor the means necessary to live with dignity, as he should, and will permit him to lay aside something in case of sickness or old age when he will no longer be physically able to continue his professorial work." *Digest*, volume 1, 655.

[2] For an interesting discussion of this problem from a non-Catholic point of view, see H. Richard Niebuhr, Daniel D. Williams, and James W. Gustafson, *The Advancement of Theological Education*, New York 1957, 57ff. Most of the comments are applicable without change to faculty members in Catholic seminaries.

³ See Kennedy, "Differentiated Discipline." His survey of seminarians' attitudes revealed that they tend to rank understanding as the most desirable quality for faculty members. "The Seminary Faculty Member: the Seminarian's View." *American Ecclesiastical Review*, volume 142, (June 1962), 390–398.

A positive way of relating with other persons has been suggested by Robert McCormick S.J.: "Relating to someone as a person means that my entire attitude and conduct reflects his total reality; and dignity—a reality and dignity founded in the fact that he is a unique individual meant to be a blueprint of no one save God in whose image and likeness he was created; possessed of an immortal soul; an intellect capable of his own original thoughts; a will capable of and responsible for his own decisions, desires, purposes; emotions capable of enthusiasms; of joy and sorrow of a unique kind; of a destiny which is so magnificent that it is describable only in terms of God himself." See "Psychosexual Development in Religious Life," a paper given at the Workshop on Psychological Development and the Religious Life, Catholic University of America.

⁴ On the caution displayed by seminarians out of their fear of not being ordained, see Sloyan's "Seminaries in America."

⁵ There are two important questions involved here. 1) The correlation of the seminarian's right of appeal and redress and the necessity of having unified and cohesive policies which are supported by the entire faculty; and 2) relationships between the seminary faculty and members of the parochial clergy. The latter are often very critical of the former and the former usually feel that the latter have little understanding of seminary problems. If the seminary faculty happens to be a religious community, the animosity may be intensified. However, even diocesan priest faculties have frequently found themselves in disagreement with their confreres in the parishes over the proper way to conduct a seminary.

⁶ I have borrowed this term from the Jesuit educational survey.

⁷ Niebuhr et al., 46, provide a penetrating discussion of this same problem in Protestant seminaries.

⁸ *Réalités*, number 158, (1964), 26.

⁹ Most Rev. George H. Speltz, "The Winona Plan: Seminary and

College," *Bulletin of the National Catholic Educational Association,* (February 1964), 1.

[10] *Ibid.,* 5–6.

[11] What Hagmaier says about the European minor seminary is pertinent:

> The particular stress the Europeans—particularly the Latins —have placed on the minor seminary stems from the cultural facts of life over there. Almost certainly, the young European is sexually far more precocious than his American cousin, and is quite likely to view heterosexual experiences far more casually. The European junior seminary is, then, as much a *protection* from the enormous pull of the local mores as it is a spiritual formation. Most Italian clergy, for example, cannot believe that a young Catholic boy in America can go to a co-ed high school without falling into irrevocable habits of sin. "Today's Religious Candidate," 111.

CHAPTER 6

[1] Hofstadter, *Anti-Intellectualism in American Life,* 136. He relies heavily on Ellis' *American Catholics and the Intellectual Life.* Both of these should be required reading for all priests. The question of Catholic intellectualism or the lack of it has, of course, been the subject of much heated debate in recent years. A very fine statement of the problem can be found in Thomas O'Dea's sociological study, *American Catholic Dilemma: An Inquiry into the Intellectual Life,* New York 1958.

Good representative thought on the subject can be found in the following:

Gustave J. Weigel S.J., "Enriching the Intellectual Life of the Catholic College," *Bulletin of the National Catholic Educational Association,* (May, 1956), 7–21.

————, "American Catholic Intellectualism: A Theologian's Reflections," *Review of Politics,* volume 19, (July, 1957), 275–307. An extensive excerpt from this article was reprinted in *Commonweal,* volume 66, 589–591.

Daniel Callahan, "After the Self-Criticism," *Commonweal*, volume 70, (April 3, 1959), 9–11.

———, "Alienation and Response," *Commonweal*, volume 72, (April 8, 1960), 31–33. A comment on this article by Michael Novak, "The Catholic Intellectual," can be found in *Commonweal*, volume 72, (May 13, 1960), 178–179.

Donald A. Campion S.J., "U.S. Catholics Come of Age," *America*, volume 100, (November 8, 1958), 164–166. This is a commentary on the O'Dea book.

After a period of quiescence, the debate has been revived again, partly in response to the publication of Hofstadter's work. Thus *Commonweal*, volume 81, (October 2, 1964), features a symposium on "The Catholic Intellectual Life: The New Debate," featuring articles by Andrew Greeley, John D. Donovan, and John W. Trent.

[2] Hofstadter, 138.

[3] Ellis, "Sermon on the Seventy-Fifth Anniversary of the Mount Angel Seminaries." There is, in fact, little or no differentiation in most seminaries in the curriculum followed by exceptional students and that followed by the average or below-average. There is usually no method of recognition for exceptional work or any formal encouragement of it.

[4] Compare this with what is stated in *Time*, art. cit., 40 in quoting a prominent Catholic layman to the effect that anticlericalism "comes when the layman feels that he knows more than the clergy." Lebreton, *History of the Primitive Church*, London 1948, volume 4, 933, points out how this intellectual rift in Catholicism gave rise, in the early Church, among the unlearned, to such oversimplified explanations of the Trinity as Modalism and Adoptionism.

[5] It is interesting that magazines intended for a wide clerical readership (as opposed to those intended for specialists) seem less original, less creative, less profound, more inclined to be "safe," and less intellectual than those destined for a combined lay-clerical readership.

[6] Eugene Burke C.S.P., "Building an Intellectual Tradition in the Seminary," *Bulletin of the National Catholic Educational Association*, (August, 1962), 58–64.

[7] See the discussion of this and other points in *America*, volume 110, (March 28, 1964), 423–426, and A. L. Bouwhuis, "Academic Accreditation for our Seminaries?" *Homiletic and Pastoral Review*, volume 60, (November, 1959), 134–140, and "Accreditation for Seminaries: Problems, Preparations, Benefits," *Catholic Library Association Proceedings*, volume 35, (1959), 135–139.

[8] See the rather remarkable criticism by William Coleman, "The Ideal Seminary," *The Priest*, (July, 1964).

[9] St. Meinrad's Seminary, Indiana, has a very fine and flourishing lay alumni association which could very well serve as a model for others throughout the country. Robert Brooks O. Praem. has stressed how seminaries generally turn their dropouts loose with little counseling and never again take any interest in them. "The Ex-Seminarian," *Ave Maria*, volume 92, (November 12, 1960), 5–10.

[10] This seems to be a rather common experience with the Graduate Record Examination in scholastic philosophy.

[11] *The Advancement of Theological Education*, already cited.

[12] "Tomorrow's Seminaries," *America*, volume 110, (January 18, 1964), 86–90.

[13] Canon 1365, #1–3.

[14] Apostolic Letter of Pius XI on seminaries and clerical studies, August 1, 1922, *Digest*, volume 1, 646–647.

On oriental studies, see the letter of the Sacred Congregation of Studies, August 28, 1929, *Digest*, volume 1.

The teaching of sacred art was reëmphasized in the letter *Tra le materie* of the Sacred Congregation of Seminaries and Universities to the Ordinaries of Italy, November 1, 1924.

Pius X reëmphasized sacred art and Gregorian Chant on November 2, 1903, *Enchiridion*, #716–717. This was repeated by Pius XI in the apostolic constitution *Divini Cultus Sanctitatem*, of December 20, 1928. *Ibid.*, #1267–1268.

The study of Canon Law was emphasized by Benedict XV in a letter to the Bishops of Italy, April 26, 1920. *Ibid.*, # 1254.

Writing to the Bishops of Italy, the Sacred Consistorial Congregation included in the theology curriculum Hebrew, patristic theology, archeology, sacred art, and chant. *Ibid.*, #872–878.

Still more details on the teaching of chant were given by the Sacred Congregation of Seminaries and Universities in an instruction of August 15, 1949, *Digest*, volume 3, 549–550.

The teaching of Sacred Scripture was spelled out in detail, together with the qualifications of the Scripture professor, by the Biblical Commission on the 13 of May, 1950. *Digest*, volume 3, 551.

The training of the professor of Church history was given in detail by a letter of Pope Pius XII on February 10, 1944. *Digest*, volume 3, 564.

See also Leo XIII in *Plane Quidem Intelligis*, of May 20, 1885, *Enchiridion*, #494, and Benedict XV, to the Bishops of Italy, April 26, 1920, *ibid.*, #1100. See also #872–878.

[15] Letter of October 9, 1921, *ibid.*, #1129. Leo XIII, *loc. cit.*, had emphasized the study of physics and mathematics for apologetic purposes, # 494. The reëmphasis on Greek, Chant, and art can be found in the letter of Pius XI on seminaries and clerical studies cited in note 15 and in the letter of Benedict XV to the Bishops of Italy cited under the same note. The latest emphasis on Latin came with *Veterum Sapientia*. See *Digest*, volume 5, 642–681.

[16] *Digest*, volume 3, 545.

[17] *The Mind of the Catholic Layman*, 132.

[18] *The Constitution on the Sacred Liturgy*, nos. 35 and 49.

CHAPTER 7

[1] An eloquent discussion of the newer concept of diocesan spirituality can be found in Jacques Leclercq, *Le prêtre devant Dieu et devant les hommes*, Tournai 1964.

[2] I have in mind particularly the schemata to be found in Adolphe Tanquerey S.S., *The Spiritual Life*, Westminster 1930, 334, 336, 337. On the necessity of mental prayer, see the statement of Pius X: "It is of the first importance that a certain time should be allotted every day for meditation on the things of eternity. No priest can omit this without being guilty of serious negligence to the detriment of his soul." Quoted *ibid.*, 326.

[3] Fichter, *Religion as an Occupation*, 233.

[4] "It is possible that a person may become so preoccupied with his own salvation that he forgets his obligation—which is particularly relevant to a professional religious functionary—to be concerned about his fellow man." *Ibid.*, 98.

[5] The *revision de vie* as practiced in the ACO is basically an attempt to think through current events in a Christian manner and to try to see them from a divine point of view.

> In a world worked upon by the Spirit, life is never neutral. What exists is always in one aspect a call of God, an event, a situation, an engagement, it always bears a hidden aspect . . . The *revision de vie* is essentially this vision of the world in the light of faith. It is not a question of psychoanalysis in common . . . not a judgment, it is a Christian outlook on the redeemed world.
>
> Each member is called on to look upon the facts of his life at home, at work, and on the move . . . The *revision de vie* proposes to see events or situations the way God sees them . . . They try to build a mentality always more impregnated with the spirit of Christ, a mentality, that is, at the same time both a way of thinking and a way of living.
> See J. Blonduelle O.P., "Foi et Revision de Vie en Action Catholique Ouvriere," *La Vie Spirituelle*, volume 103, (December 1960), 529–547. On its use among priests, see Leclercq, *Le prêtre*, 134–136.

[6] "In seminaries and houses of religious, clerics shall be given a liturgical formation to their spiritual life. For this they will need proper direction, so that they may be able to understand the sacred rites and take part in them whole-heartedly; and they will also need personally to celebrate the sacred mysteries, as well as popular devotions which are imbued with the spirit of the liturgy." *The Constitution on the Sacred Liturgy*, no. 17.

[7] For suggestions on practical participation, see:
John Symon, "Liturgy in the Seminary," *Furrow*, volume 40, (March, 1963), 148–160.

"Suggestions for Seminaries," *Worship*, volume 36, (September, 1962), 519–523.

The Mass: Pastoral Directory, Montreal Diocesan Liturgical Commission 1962.

[8] *The Constitution on the Sacred Liturgy*, no. 89.

CHAPTER 8

[1] This opinion can be found in the *Time* article previously noted, 40. See also Philip Scharper, "Speculations," *The Critic*, volume 23, (October-November, 1964), 38–39.

[2] A summary of this concept of obedience can be found in the article by Raymond Beaudry, "The Mystery of Obedience," *American Ecclesiastical Review*, volume 147, (September, 1962), 174ff.

[3] Sacred Congregation of Seminaries and Universities, *Circular Letter on the Centenary of the Death of the Curé of Ars*, 4.

[4] *Religion as an Occupation*, 91–92.

[5] *Pacem in Terris*, America Press 1963, paragraph 46ff.

[6] Fichter, *Religion as an Occupation*, passim. Karl Rahner, "Reflections on Obedience," *Cross Currents*, volume 10, (Fall, 1960), 363–374.

Andrew Greeley, "Fraternal Authority in the Church," *Homiletic and Pastoral Review*, volume 64, (April, 1964), 561–570. Greeley's use of the terms "fraternal" and "paternal" to contrast the exercise of a more trusting and liberal type of authority with that which is despotic and deadening caused some confusion to his readers. Close reading of the article will, I think, convince anyone of the soundness of Greeley's approach. Unfortunately, the comments by T. Lincoln Bouscare S.J., (August, 1964, 921–926) miss much of this point. Bouscaren rests his case on questionable grounds when he assumes that current discontent in the Church is restricted to a "minority." He also assumes the divine nature of each single command of a superior without even noting the theological difficulties involved in this approach, difficulties which Rahner exposes very clearly in his treatment of the subject.

See also Eugene Kennedy, "Differentiated Discipline in the Seminary."

⁷ There is a certain amount of confusion about the precise meaning of this term "blind" obedience. Here I am referring to the way in which this is *ordinarily practiced*, that is, the subject is expected to be entirely passive in receiving directives from superiors, and that outside of cases of obvious sin there is to be no questioning of them by the subject.

⁸ 567.

⁹ 367–373.

¹⁰ *Ibid.*

¹¹ *Ibid.*

¹² 562.

¹³ 564.

¹⁴ *Ibid.*

¹⁵ Art. cit.

¹⁶ See Greeley, *op. cit.*, 562.

¹⁷ Pius XII, *Menti Nostrae*, in *The Popes and the Priesthood*, St. Meinrad 1953, paragraph 84.

¹⁸ A summary of this stage of development can be found in the Jesuit educational survey referred to above and O'Doherty's "Emotional Development of the Ecclesiastical Student."

¹⁹ "If young men—especially those who have entered the seminary at an early age—are educated in an environment too isolated from the world, they may, on leaving the seminary, find serious difficulty in their relations with either the ordinary people or the educated laity, and it may happen that they adopt a misguided and false attitude toward the faithful or that they consider their training in in an unfavorable light." Paragraph 86.

²⁰ Pius XI, *Quadragesimo Anno*, Acta Apostolicae Sedis, 1931, 203.

²¹ "The second element [in psychosexual maturity], increased auto-determination, needs much attention. For religious life, especially early religious life, by training groupwise to a 'foreign ascetical ideal,' risks producing conforming automata—especially if we reflect on the early and immature age of entrance into religious life. The sooner the acts and practices of religious life can convert from 'pressures' into freely chosen acts, the better. This means one thing to me: early communication of responsibility. I propose that

we religious have been seriously defective in this regard." McCormick, "Psychosexual Development in Religious Life."

22 ". . . Directors of seminaries must use moderation in the employment of coercive means, gradually lightening the system of rigorous control and restrictions as the boys grow older, by helping the boys themselves to stand on their own feet and to feel responsibility for their own actions." Paragraph 84.

APPENDIX

1 What has been written on the subject of seminary dropouts has been for the most part rather superficial. Only Robert Brooks O. Praem. has used the logical approach of interviewing the former seminarians themselves, but his purpose was more a study of their personality problems and their adaptations than of their reasons for changing vocations. Nevertheless, the work he has done is uniformly valuable and enlightening. His conclusions can be found summarized in the Ave Maria article already cited; this was based on the material that he gathered for his doctoral dissertation on former seminarians (University of Notre Dame 1959). Bishop John J. Wright's standard article and speech, "Perseverance in the Seminary: Problems and Remedies," American Ecclesiastical Review, volume 47, (August, 1962), 73–87, suffers from a serious lack of updating and acquaintance with the problems of contemporary seminarians. His most interesting point, acedia, receives cursory treatment.

R. Klaver's article, "Why Do Seminarians Leave the Seminary," already cited, contains a very good summary of the elements that make up a vocation. He rejects most of the standard reasons given for nonperseverance as extrinsic to the question, and says that the basic cause is a lack of commitment to the program of holiness offered by the seminary. He does not seem to think that the so-called extrinsic causes may impede this commitment and hence be very important after all.

James P. McKay, "The Devil with Vocations: Seminary Dropouts," Emmanuel, volume 68, (August, 1962), 301–304, is typical of the fundamentalist approach to the question. For him, the cause of nonperseverance is precisely what the title says, the devil. With all due respect, I think that McKay fails to credit the devil with working through secondary causes. If his thesis were accepted literally, the logical solution would be exorcism.

[2] Ellis, in his sermon at the Mount Angel Seminaries, has some cogent thoughts on the subject:

> Has there not been too often a failure to counterbalance the warning against the altogether real danger of intellectual pride with the equally real danger of intellectual sloth? A year or more ago a seminary rector was heard to remark that he did not encourage A students because they were usually troublemakers. A remark of this kind, it is to be hoped, represents no more than an isolated eccentricity, for had the superiors of Thomas Aquinas, Robert Bellarmine, and Jean Mabillon reasoned in this fashion, what a grievous loss would have been sustained by Christian thought and scholarship?

[3] See Bernardin Goebel O.F.M. Cap., *Seven Steps to the Altar*, New York 1963.

Many parish priests find it difficult to believe that a young man can leave the seminary merely because he does not want to be a priest. No matter what the reasons for a choice, the young man still does have a free choice as to his vocation, and many make use of this freedom to decide against the priesthood, even though they appear to have all the necessary and desirable qualities.